THE CHURCHES
PICTURED BY 'PUNCH'

It is the heart that is not yet sure of God that is afraid to laugh in his presence

—GEORGE McDONALD

THE CHURCHES
PICTURED BY 'PUNCH'

BY

A. L. DRUMMOND

PATENT PULPITS

THE EPWORTH PRESS
(EDGAR C. BARTON)
25-35 City Road, London, E.C.1

PRINTED IN GREAT BRITAIN
BY WESTERN PRINTING SERVICES LTD., BRISTOL

TO

The Rev. A. M. McIVER, B.D.
MINISTER OF THE CHURCH OF SCOTLAND

WHOSE REVERENT USE OF WHOLESOME HUMOUR HAS
REFRESHED MANY A HOLIDAY-MAKER WHO HAS 'SAT
UNDER HIM' IN THE PARISH KIRK OF HOPE PARK
ST. ANDREWS

CONTENTS

V

ILLUSTRATIONS

With grateful acknowledgements to the Proprietors of *Punch* and the Rev. D. Wallace Duthie, author of *The Church in the Pages of 'Punch'* (Smith, Elder, 1912)— unfortunately now out of print

THE BIOGRAPHER[1] of Bishop Walsham How, who modestly claimed to dig up only a few spadefuls of ecclesiastical humour from the twelfth to the eighteenth centuries, tells how a certain Dr. Mountain, son of a beggar, became Bishop of Durham. George the Second, searching for a new Archbishop of York, consulted Mountain, who replied: 'Hadst thou faith as a grain of mustard seed thou wouldst say to this *mountain*' (laying his hands on his heart), '"Be removed and cast into the See"!' George the Second laughed heartily and gave Mountain the See of York.

Would that in every age there were a chronicler to keep record of the lighter side of Church life, and to restore to due proportion the controversies so often magnified by ecclesiastics! The year that gave birth to Edward the Peacemaker saw the first appearance of *Punch* the mirth-maker. Since 1841 the national *Charivari* has kept a weekly record of British history—sung in epigram, scored in verse, sketched in cartoon, salted with satire, and seasoned with jest.[2] Now that the late Professor Stephen Leacock has given *Humour* an academic niche in *The Home University Library*, we are all the more alive to its real significance in social, political, and religious history. In Benham's *Book of Quotations* there are over one hundred and forty 'famous words from *Punch*'. This paper may well be described as an index of the English mind, a weathercock showing the way

[1] F. D. How, *Clerical Humour of Olden Time* (Pitman, 1908).
[2] M. H. Spielmann, *The History of 'Punch'* (1895). C. L. Graves, *Mr. Punch's History of Modern England* (New York, c. 1920).

9

the wind blows.[1] In his youth, *Mr. Punch* was not content to be a jester. He was a preacher, a moralist, a social reformer. On the one hand, he was an idealist, standing for the rights of under-privileged classes and oppressed nationalities: on the other, he was the unsparing foe of cant, Pharisaism, and fanaticism. In religion he was a veritable John Bull, outspoken in abuse of 'Puseyism and Popery'. Indeed, he identified himself with the prejudices of the average Englishman so wholeheartedly that the Rt. Hon. G. W. E. Russell declared that his attitude toward the English Church has been a 'Comedy of Errors'.

The Rev. D. Wallace Duthie in his invaluable and detailed study, *The Church in the Pages of 'Punch'* (Smith, Elder, 1912), has given a fascinating panorama of Early-Victorian religion. In the centre of the picture is the Church of England, still hampered by the abuses of the eighteenth century—pluralities, non-residence, political and social privilege. *Mr. Punch* smites these evils hip-and-thigh, but for all that remains an incorrigible Erastian: to allow the Church self-government is to give scope for Popish and Puseyite propaganda; nor has he much sympathy with Evangelicals within the Establishment and Nonconformists outside. By the later Victorian period, *Mr. Punch* has mellowed considerably, and no longer takes sides so unblushingly in current controversies; he rather seeks to play the part of an umpire among heated religionists, advocating fair play all round. After the first world war, he loses interest in theological and ecclesiastical issues, and sees the Church mainly through the remarks of parsons, vergers, aged parishioners, and Sunday-school teachers. The Church is no longer a national institution of cardinal importance; it is rather a social institution that still lingers in the swiftly changing scene.

[1] cf. Amy Cruse, *The Victorians and their Books*, Chapter 18, 'Punch' (Allen & Unwin, 1935).

Without further delay, then, let us turn to *Mr. Punch's* commentary on a century of Church life, mainly in England.

There pass before us first, movements to be assessed and criticized—Tractarianism, Romanism, Ritualism. Then comes the processional of English clergy—rich bishops and incumbents of fat livings to be censured, poor curates to be pitied, missionaries to be ridiculed. Doctrinal sparks fly fast and furious when Churchmen—High, Low, and Broad—come into conflict. Church services and their setting, preachers and congregations are now surveyed. The English Establishment occupies the centre of the picture; in the background there lurk a few Dissenters and Scottish Presbyterians.

'As the crackling of thorns under a pot, so is the laughter of a fool.' Traditional religion has been guilty of dourness rather than levity. 'I sat not in the company of the sportive, nor made merry with them' (Jeremiah 15$_{17}$, tr. A. R. Gordon). Yet even that 'tamed cynic', Ecclesiastes, admitted that there is 'a time to laugh', as well as 'a time to weep'. It is not good for the Christian to be always serious, as an individual, or in corporate capacity. Every parson, vestryman, elder or deacon would be the better for surveying the ecclesiastical scene through the window of humour. He would see controversy in better proportions. He would find officialism, professionalism, and hypocrisy deflated. He would experience a relaxation of life's tension, and discover that kindly character is often nearer the spirit of Christ than conventional creed. *Punch* fulfils the function outlined by the eighteenth-century poet, Thomas Tickell:

> Fight virtue's cause,
> Stand up in wit's defence,
> Win us from vice,
> And laugh us into sense.

I

THE first number of *Punch* appeared in 1841. Four years later the Tractarian leaders—Newman, Ward, and Faber—seceded to the Church of Rome. Those who preferred to remain within the English Church, faithful to the Oxford Movement of 1833, received no sympathy from *Punch*. Keble did not interest him; it was Pusey who appeared as the evil genius of the High Church heresy. A cartoon of 1850 represents 'Pussey' snatching chestnuts out of the fire for the Papal Monkey in whose arms he is held. *Punch* merely echoed prevailing public opinion when he branded as casuistry the Tractarian argument that the best way to meet Roman claims was to put forth a counter-claim; the plea that the English Church was no creature of the State but a branch of the Holy Catholic Church, rejoicing in all the privileges of Apostolic Succession. *Punch* rejected this *via media* between Rome and Protestantism in much the same way as *John Bull* eliminated another compromise —the second-class railway carriage. Pusey was bidden to go to Rome in 1860, though he had proved a good Anglican since the agitation of 1850, and was satisfied with a minimum of ritual. His only honest course lay across the Tiber —and he would probably receive from the Pope a lucrative appointment in the Inquisition! When he turned from Rome to Dissent and made overtures to the Wesleyan Conference (rejected in 1868), prim 'Miss Methodist' replied in a vixenish manner: 'I don't want to go to church at all, and if I did, I'm sure I wouldn't go with you.' Whereupon the Wesleyan Conference adapted a popular song of the day to the situation:

You offer one hand to the Papal band,
    And the other to us extend,
Can you really hope that we and the Pope
    Can acknowledge a mutual friend?
You tell us our bark is not an ark,
    We don't believe that's true,
We'd trust a raft before your craft,
    Just paddle your own canoe.

Punch had no words of respect when Pusey died in 1882.
It is all the more surprising that he had no comment to
make when Newman made his dramatic exodus to the
Church of Rome in 1845. The devout, questing spirit of
this storm-tossed soul woke no generous response in the
heart of the complacent, insular Englishman of this period;
his views were 'Newmania'; even his *Apologia* (1864) did
not still controversy, as we might reasonably expect. When
Newman returns to 'the apostate city of Oxford' after many
years, *Punch* describes the Cardinal's shudder when he sees
the Martyrs' Memorial, but when he revisits his old college,
a kindlier feeling blossoms in the verse:

Once more in Oriel face to face
    With scenes to ancient memories due,
Is't a NEW man in the old place,
    Or is't an old man in the new?

More familiar to the readers of *Punch* was the worn,
ascetic face and piercing look of Manning, the Anglican
Archdeacon, who was not content to slip quietly into the
Roman Communion, but was determined to make the
Church of his adoption once more a power in England.
Surprise and disappointment are registered on his imperious
features when he, 'Chambermaid of the Vatican', finds that
the High Church leaders decline to be lighted upstairs by
him (1869). The following year Mark Lemon, who had
controlled the destiny of *Punch* since 1841, passed to his

rest. As Mr. Duthie informs us significantly: 'a Roman Catholic sat in his seat.' Henceforth, Manning is treated no longer as a showman and 'star' propagandist, but with marked respect as a great Englishman whose personality impressed the whole nation. In his later years, he distinguished himself as the ambassador of peace, intervening between Capital and Labour. *Punch* does not forget the personal decision which changed the whole course of his career; in 1882 he pictures the Roman Cardinal seeing in the looking-glass the Anglican Bishop he might have become.

Another Cardinal, Dr. Wiseman, who was head of the Irish hierarchy, fared far worse than Manning. From 1850 till 1865 he was the constant butt of *Punch*, grotesquely represented as a hawker of relics. He complained, not without reason, that '*Punch*, the playful companion of everyone's railway journey, had taken to preach and be a saint and had lost all his good humour'. What was the cause of this? Cardinal Wiseman, encouraged by secessions from the Anglican Church, had painted the prospects of Catholicism in such bright colours that the Pope directed the restoration of the title of Bishop, which had been disused since the English Reformation in favour of colourless 'Vicars Apostolic'; their districts now became Sees (1850). Wiseman promulgated a pastoral letter 'given out of the Flaminian Gate of Rome'; read in the London churches of the Roman Communion, it announced: 'Catholic England has been restored to the Orbit in the Ecclesiastical firmament . . . and begins anew its course of regularly adjusted action round the centre of gravity, the source of jurisdiction, of light, and of vigour.'

To indulge in this rhetoric was utterly tactless. Not only had the National Church lost some of her finest clergy, but wealthy landowners had gone Catholic and were busy endowing churches, colleges, and monasteries. For over

ten years Pugin had been renewing the face of Catholic
England by his ambitious Gothic churches and cathedrals.
English Catholicism was no longer a picturesque survival
consisting of old families worshipping with their tenants and
a few country-tradesmen in obscure chapels. 'The quality'
were gradually coming over to Rome via Tractarianism,
and the quantity was supplied in the persons of thousands
of impoverished Irish, who swarmed into the cities and
even the country towns of England during the 'hungry
forties'. Pius the Ninth and Cardinal Wiseman felt that
they were ushering in a second spring of Catholicism:[1] this
accounts for the hysterical outburst of Protestant indigna-
tion. Patriotism, piety, and politics armed themselves with
Reformation slogans against the possible restoration of fire
and rack. The 'Ecclesiastical Titles Bill' was passed under
pressure of public opinion, and the historic English principle reaffirmed: 'The Pope hath no jurisdiction in these
islands.' *Punch* pictured the Pontiff as a Guy Fawkes with
attendant conspirators, and as Goliath trembling before
David (Lord John Russell). Even after the 'No Popery'
scare had passed, Pius the Ninth was pursued with ridicule
and invective. This was not altogether mere prejudice; the
Pontiff was the centre of European reaction. He held up
the cause of Italian Unity, and was the deadly enemy of
Garibaldi (idolized in England). Moreover, the Papal
States were wretchedly governed by ecclesiastics; Rome
swarmed with beggars; no Protestant Church was tolerated.
When the flag of united Italy flew over the Holy City in
1870, *Punch* was jubilant; but in 1877 he chats genially
with Pius the Ninth—no longer a villain, but 'a blameless,
genial, gentle old man'. Much ill humour might have been
avoided had the Pontiff not been misled by his Cardinal in
1850.

[1] Denis Gwynn, *The Second Spring* (1818-52) (Burns Oates,
1945).

With Pius, Wiseman tries
To lay us under ban.
O Pius, man unwise,
O impious Wiseman!

Punch was obsessed by 'the scarlet woman of Babylon'. He 'saw red' whenever he caught sight of monks, nuns, and Jesuits. His spirit was quite that of Protestant zealots like Kensit and Jacob Primmer. His attitude was particularly provocative where Irishmen were concerned; he pictures the Irish Catholic bound hand and foot, while his priest refuses to marry or bury him until he registers his parliamentary vote at ecclesiastical bidding. Yet *Punch* had even less sympathy with 'those Brummagem Papists, the Puseyites', poor relations of the Roman Catholics, traitors within the gate. Our statesman must take a strong stand against them—unlike Lord John Russell, who is represented as a boy chalking 'No Popery' on the wall and then bolting. The various phases of the High Church controversy are reflected in the pages of *Punch*. A landmark was the 'Gorham Case' (1850). Phillpotts, Bishop of Exeter, refused to institute Mr. Gorham, an Evangelical, to a Devonshire parish, owing to his views on Baptismal Regeneration. The ecclesiastical 'Court of Arches' supported the Bishop, but its judgement was reversed by the Privy Council. This Erastian action caused Manning and others to leave the Church of England; but *Punch* was all for Gorham:

The Pope, his compassion for sinners to prove,
  Sends Bulls without mercy to bore 'em,
Our Phillpotts to shew his more fatherly love,
  Refuses permission to Gore 'em.

The same year *Punch* published a cartoon, 'The Puseyite Moth and the Roman Candle', with the advice: 'Fly away, silly moth'. Mr. Bennett, of St. Paul's, Knightsbridge, refused to fly away, but persisted in his innovation of choral services. Prosecuted for maintaining the Real Presence in 1869, he had to leave London despite his acquittal and settled at Frome: *Punch* considered that his heart lay rather in Rome, but was too fond of the 'loaves and fishes' of an English Church living. Thoroughly unselfish was Mackonochie, the Anglo-Catholic priest who carried the Gospel into the worst quarters of the East End. Ritual disturbances led to prosecution before the Court of Arches; this time the verdict was not reversed, but upheld by the Privy Council: 'And now, Mr. Mackonochie, what next?' But this 'defiant jackdaw' cared nothing for Archbishop Tait, and paid no attention to *Punch*'s pointed question: 'Under which king, Bezonian? speak, or die. The Church of England by law established, or the Church of which in this country the top sawyer is Cardinal Manning?' Another figure much in the pages of *Punch* was the Rev. Mr. Tooth of Hatcham—'The unsound tooth that can't be stopped'. The severest persecution and riots in his church[1] failed to divert him from his principles; he was even imprisoned. At last *Punch* announced in 1877: 'The Rev. Mr. Tooth has vacated his benefice for conscience' sake. He deserves to be called Honourable and Reverend now.'

The earlier 'Puseyism' blossomed forth into 'ritualism'. Ceremonial was now the fashion. Martin Tupper was at one with *Punch* in his scorn for 'Flirts of the chancel! ye milliner priests, decked in your laces and satin-bound hems'. Ascetic priests in the West End exercised a growing influence over young ladies. 'Confession or Cremorne, my lady?' inquires an 1858 footman at the carriage door. A High Church manual, *The Priest in Absolution*, obtained much publicity and notoriety in 1877, and roused Protestant sentiment as nothing had done since the Papal Aggression

---

[1] Baring-Gould in his *Church Revival* (Methuen) gives an entertaining account of some of these episodes, with several cartoons reproduced.

B

of 1850. *Punch* pictures a Father Confessor as 'A wolf in sheep's clothing', and turns him off the doorstep of a disgusted matron: 'Whenever you see any of these sneaking scoundrels about, mam, just send for me, I'll deal with them, never fear.' He had not changed views expressed some nine years earlier: 'What is there to prevent the Pope from giving Ritualists gone over to Rome a dispensation to remain ostensibly in the English Church, and there act the part of decoy ducks in regard to geese?'

On the lighter side, he recommended such preparations as 'Achromaticon' and 'Macerative Elixir'—warranted to produce in a few days a personal appearance not to be distinguished from years of asceticism. Abstinence from meat on fast days could be offset by a more refined cuisine, though this may have its difficulties—as in 1851, when the Lenten menu drives the rector's cook to throw up her hands and her situation.

Passing to more serious matters, one is struck by *Punch's* severity to the bench of bishops between the forties and the seventies. Erastian as he is, he wields the scourge with relentless vigour. Respect for 'the cloth' does not restrain him from referring to the Bishops of Oxford and Durham as 'Soapy and Cheesy'! One obvious objection to the 'Lords Spiritual' was the fact that they were the defenders of class privilege, the enemies of all reform; they were not even appreciated by the Lords Temporal. Chancellor Westbury announced in debate that he had never known a bishop who could be said to have any mind at all. *Punch* was of that opinion, and when the Bishop of Oxford applied for a 'faculty', he asked how many Bishops have faculties to spare? Chosen on grounds of social standing, as 'safe men', or as party nominees, the prelates were almost as grossly over-paid as their latitudinarian predecessors in the eighteenth century; and almost as lazy. The Archbishop of York drew £40,000 annually from his See, and the Bishop of Durham £20,000 (till the Act of 1856). Seven or eight

Irish Protestant prelates, who died in 1845, left behind them about £200,000 apiece. In connexion with a Parliamentary Inquiry into the state of Episcopal incomes, a cartoon represents the Bishops wildly stampeding before the attack of Mr. Horsman, M.P., carrying away in their aprons as much of their plunder as possible! *Punch* could have strengthened his case if he had noted that at this period 'the aggregate income of all the sixteen Archbishops and seventy-one Bishops of France fell short of the revenue of the present Protestant Bishop of London, and exceeded only by a trifle that of the Bishop of Durham'.[1]

'Baths for those who require them' (1844). An English prelate in full canonicals flounders about in the dubious company of rascally lawyers and the like. The Bishops were not content to live delicately in 'purple and fine linen', while Lazarus rotted in rags during the 'hungry forties'; they provided unblushingly for their relatives out of the Church's 'livings'. Even Evangelical bishops had no conscience in this matter; Villiers, appointed by Lord Shaftesbury to the See of Durham, lost no time in appointing his son-in-law to Haughton-le-Skern (worth £1,300), and ignored a deputation of churchwardens who requested that a portion of this revenue be allocated to Darlington, with its growing population. Cheese was the name of the presentee, only ordained three years before. *Punch* at once dubbed the Bishop 'Cheesy', and excused his patronage by remarking, 'Cheese always comes before *dessert*'. Nepotism was aggravated by Pluralism. The Bishop of Durham had presented four benefices to one man within five years, and one of these livings was worth £2,000 a year. *Punch* was therefore able to announce the exact location of the Garden of Eden, for such was the name of the fortunate incumbent! Perhaps the crowning scandal was a Church official in a

[1] See D. Woodruff's 'The Abbé Migne' in *Great Catholics*, p. 370 (London, 1938).

southern diocese who received £9,000 as Registrar (for work entirely done by deputies), £3,000 as a Canon of Canterbury, and another £1,000 from several rectories. No doubt he was truly grateful to his loving father, the Archbishop of Canterbury. 'To him that hath shall be given.'

Du Maurier was appointed to the staff of *Punch* by Mark Lemon in 1865, and introduced a more kindly note into *Punch's* opinion of prelates. 'Bishop-baiting' had had its day, and the old abuses gradually disappeared from the sixties onwards. Du Maurier's bishop is still outwardly impressive, but he is no longer feared. 'Of whom am I even afraid?' he asks his page. 'The missus, my Lord' (a cartoon that at once reminds us of Bishop and Mrs. Proudie). At a meeting of the Church of England Temperance Society a clerical speaker is introducing an unattractive and be-whiskered, aproned specimen: 'And, Ladies and Gentlemen, let me point out to you, in these days when the activity of the Church is so often called into question, that our revered Diocesan could never be called an "Ornamental Bishop"!' Familiarity is apt to breed contempt. By the eighties Bishops no longer made a point of travelling in state on every occasion; they sometimes made their way by bus and rail. Charles Keene pictures one of them in a third-class carriage, asked by a drunken man: 'Are you a curate?' 'I was once.' 'Ah! Drink again!' It was no doubt good for high ecclesiastics to rub shoulders with the plain man, but democratic patronage can be almost as distasteful as brickbats. One result of coming off an official pedestal is to forfeit the reverence of juveniles. 'The Bishop's kind,' said a little girl returning home from the Palace (where he had tried to come down to her level), 'but, oh, mummy, the brains of a kitten!' A boy says curtly to his Lordship: 'I have swopped you [i.e. the signature on a post card] for two New Zealanders.' Then there is the lad who explains that a Bishop's visitation is 'an affliction sent from heaven'!

Coming to personalities, we find that *Punch*, like Carlyle, had no liking for Bishop Samuel Wilberforce of Oxford. For a quarter of a century 'Soapy Sam' was an offence: partly owing to a certain smug pietism which he had inherited from his father, the great Evangelical philanthropist, partly owing to his showmanship in patronizing and promoting the Oxford Movement; he was certainly an 'opportunist'. The Rev. J. C. Hardwick has portrayed this 'Good Churchman' in his entertaining biography *Lawn Sleeves* (Oxford, 1933). In 'Stanzas to St. Sam' *Punch* censured him for his uncompromising opposition to the Divorce Bill of 1857:

> Tell me, Bishop, tell me why
>   If you had your little will,
> You'd keep bound in cruel tie,
>   Injured spouse and false wife still.

When the Oxford clergy appealed to Bishop Wilberforce against the daring 'Modernism' of the Bampton Lecturer, *Punch* took the side of Hampden, and stood by him when Lord John Russell insisted on his appointment (despite ecclesiastical protests) as Bishop of Hereford. Theological liberals are often incorrigible conservatives in other ways, and when Hampden abused patronage as much as any old-fashioned Church-and-State man, Punch had to correct him so severely that he wobbled on his pedestal.

Wilberforce was a great believer in 'The Church Overseas'. Little did he imagine that in promoting Colonial Bishoprics he was nursing a viper that would sting sound Churchmanship. Colenso had not been appointed Bishop of Natal for more than a few years before he attacked the historicity of the early Genesis narratives (1862). His doubts had been awakened by a converted Zulu who asked him how the animals got on in the ark, if beasts of prey were admitted. As a mathematician, he began to question the statistics of the Old Testament. Wilberforce, who was not without a sense of humour, said that he was jealous of

Moses for writing a 'book of numbers' before him! Bishop
Gray of Capetown, an extreme High Churchman, launched
against Colenso 'the greater excommunication'. Colenso
appealed to the Privy Council and his case was sustained.
Punch took up the cause of Natal's injured bishop against
Wilberforce and Gray (who were supported by 'the religious
world', High and Low thirsting for the condemnation of
'the bad bishop'). It appeared in this instance Erastianism
safeguarded ecclesiastical justice. *Punch's* last mention of
the Bishop of Natal was in 1875, wishing him good luck;
he had done splendid work in advocating the rights of the
native races. Another Colonial bishop, Selwyn, who started
pioneer work in New Zealand in 1841, the same year that
the London *Charivari* was founded, made a stronger appeal
to our national humorist than most missionaries. He felled
forests, swam rivers, and tamed cannibals. 'Every inch a
man' was *Punch's* verdict.

When Gladstone nominated Dr. Fraser Bishop of Man-
chester, he appointed a social reformer who took an intimate
interest in the life of a modern industrial community. He
was quite a new type of prelate and *Punch* approved of him.
When Tait became Bishop of London in 1857, he forsook
the West End in order to make friends with the poor of
Bethnal Green. Again *Punch* approved. As the son of a
Scots Presbyterian, Tait was an anti-ritualist. In a cartoon
of 1858 he admonishes a group of clergy holding vases of
flowers, crosses, and candles: 'You must not bring your
playthings into Church, little men.' As Archbishop of
Canterbury he sponsored Disraeli's measure to limit ritual
elaboration (1874) and was greeted metrically by *Punch*:

> The Church should thank you, Tait—in time it will,
> For your sagacious Public Worship Bill.

The Diocese of Exeter was much to the fore in Victorian
times. We have heard of Phillpotts, that doughty High
Church persecutor of Gorham (1850). An early cartoon

represents him answering a question: 'Please, which is Popery, and which is Puseyism?' with: 'Whichever you like my little dear.' Very different was his successor, Dr. Temple, one of the contributors to the Broad Church *Essays and Reviews*. The Chapter of Exeter Cathedral, roused by the High Church leaders, was unwilling to elect Temple formally as the government's nominee. But *Punch* was sure that he would 'turn out the best bishop they've ever had in the West'. One of his activities was the promotion of Temperance—something new for a Bishop. The temptation of a pun could not be resisted, in this connexion:

> How keenly these Exeter Bishops endeavour
> To prove they belong to such different lots,
> As the creed of the old one was 'Phillpotts for ever'
> The cry of the new one is 'Never fill pots'.

FOOD FOR THOUGHT

MINISTER (*much gratified*). 'And so, Saunders, you think that we ministers ought to get larger stipends.'

SAUNDERS. 'Ay. Ye see we wad get a better class o' men!'

II

WHEN *PUNCH* came into the world in 1841, eighteenth-century conditions still persisted in the English Church, only gradually undergoing modification. The Oxford Movement had not yet had time to leaven Anglicanism thoroughly. The average clergyman was a kindly and respectable member of society, sharing the social position, habits, and prejudices of the ruling class. He was usually on the local Bench, and described accordingly by a Frenchman in his 'Simple Notes on England' as 'a magistrate who preaches'. *Punch* censures the heavy fines imposed by clerical magistrates on poachers, but like Trollope, has a soft heart for clerical sportsmen. When Parson 'Jack' Russell of Swymbridge, master of foxhounds, rode forty miles to dine with his friends at the age of 85, *Punch* was among his admirers; but he covered with ridicule the priest who (before 1870) justified his following of hounds in Lent by dressing in black. The sporting parson was fast dying out (apart from fishing), though 'muscular Christianity' had brought in a new type of athletic clergyman, addicted to boxing, cricket, and football. Parsons of all schools were still assiduous in looking after 'the inner man', though they were often perfunctory in 'doing duty' in the parish. The table preferences of the two great ecclesiastical parties was well illustrated by Keene's drawing of a butler consulting the Squire about a clerical dinner party. ' 'Igh or Low, Sir?' 'Why do you ask, Prodgers?' 'Well, you see, sir, the 'Igh drinks most wine, and the Low eats most vittles, and I must perwide accordin'.' The old type of convivial parson was disappearing; here and there a 'die-hard' sang:

> An old and sound divine . . .
> I go on drinking daily,
> And this is always my advice
> O stick to Port and Paley!

Even in the fifties the general level of clerical efficiency
was not high. In 1854 a Minor Canon of St. Paul's left his
church in the country four Sundays out of five without
service, the churchwardens having to read Prayers the
fifth Sunday; and all the time there was a cholera epidemic
in the village: but *Punch* is more concerned about the doings
of certain black sheep when absent. He quotes a case in the
diocese of Peterborough (1844), the Bishop being unable to
take any action against the offender because the offence was
committed in Paris. There was no law of spiritual extradi-
tion. Until 1892, drunken or immoral priests, having
served their term of banishment or imprisonment, were
legally able to return to their scandalized parishes and
resume their ministry. 'Only after a long struggle did the
Act become law', says the Rev. D. W. Duthie significantly.

What happened to superannuated parsons? An old
gentleman, investigating an old church, observed: 'Very
charming old sedilia you have here'.—'Yes, sir,' replied
the old woman caretaker, 'you ain't the fust as 'as admired
'em. That's where the clergymen used to sit in the order
of their senility.'

Coming to the momentous question of how the clergy
were to be assisted in their arduous duties, we are surprised
to find that the parson's wife[1] does not appear in the earlier
days of *Punch* as regularly as we might expect. The general
impression is the presence of an energetic and well-meaning
'parsonette', whose activities are not always fully appreciated. 'When the gentleman's haffable, the lady's
'aughty', says the village philosopher. A little girl gives

[1] See Margaret H. Watt, *The History of the Parson's Wife*
(Faber, 1943).

'Vicar' as the masculine of 'Vixen'. 'I don't believe in a married clergy' explains the High Church wife of a certain rector, who on principle attended the neighbouring church of a celibate priest.

Among the parson's occasional helpers appears the 'locum tenens'. An inquirer asks for the health of a sick rector in 1884 : 'Has he got a locum tenens?' 'No, sir,' says the servant, 'same old pain in the back.' A few years later *Punch* was able to convict that uncompromisingly Evangelical paper, the *Record*, of advertising for a very High Churchman indeed: 'Locum tenens, good preacher, 300 feet high, and usual fees'. His weekend entertainment must have been a problem, even before the days of rationing.

It was the curate, however, who was the parson's mainstay: 'a sort of journeyman parson ready to job a pulpit by the day.' In the early days of *Punch* curates frequently ran the parishes of absentee clergy; they were the 'Toilers of the See' (to adapt the title of Victor Hugo's novel). A highly endowed State Church, staffed by opulent bishops and portly rectors, was run by 'sweated labour'; and this 'mendicant order' was dependent on charity for 'Secondhand Canonicals'. To take two instances from Cumberland: the living of St. Cuthbert's, Carlisle, was worth £1,500 a year, while the curate's wages were £5 16s. 8d.; Warwick Wetheral, £1,600, and £52. When the first Pan-Anglican Synod met, *Punch* scanned its programme and pictured an anxious wife asking her husband: 'Any help for our difficulties, dear?' 'Oh, no, we poor curates are not even mentioned.' The Poor Clergy Relief Society reported in 1880 that no less than 5,000 curates received under an average salary of £80, while the same number of beneficed clergy got only £150. When one considers that a great many were family men, like Trollope's 'Rev. Mr. Quiverful', we can understand their miserable condition. Low pay was by no means the reward of light work. In 1853 a curate in a Lichfield village was expected to 'read daily prayers, take evening Communion, be responsible for day, night, and Sunday-schools, have good health, and preach three or four times on Sunday'. One 'kept a curate' as one kept a maid-of-all-work. An advertisement of 1870 required: 'curate, stipend £150, second year £120; to undertake the whole duty when the Rector is away, about nine months in the year, and to superintend the making of the Rector's hay.' The improvement in the status of the curate owed much to the philanthropic activity of *Punch*, who kept an eye on official statistics and advertisements. Toward the close of the century the curate profited by the more humane and democratic attitude that prevailed. He became the darling of the drawing-room, and accordingly presumptuous. 'And do you like the pulpit, Mr. Auriol?' asks a fair parishioner. 'I do not. Er—it hides too much of the figure and I like every shake of the surplice to tell!'

Punch did much to reform other clerical abuses besides the exploitation of curates. One of these institutions (now almost obsolete) was the 'Proprietary Chapel', satirized by Thackeray in *The Newcomes*. An advertisement from *The Times* (1852) reads: 'A young gentleman of family, evangelically disposed, and to whom salary is no object, may hear of a cure in a fashionable West End congregation, by addressing the Rev. A. M. O. at Hatchard's, Bookseller, Piccadilly.' In December 1845 Leech portrays the kind of religion to be found at these chapels connected with the Establishment.

At one door an obsequious sidesman, whiskered and ringleted, admits fine ladies; at the other, a Dickensian beadle in cocked hat and scarlet cloak drives off (with a cross-tipped staff) childhood, age, and poverty. In 1844 *Punch* offered 'some modest proposals for a Proprietary Chapel'. Every pew must be let at a high rent to keep the place select; the clergyman, ingratiating in manner, attractive in appearance, and engaged at a high salary, must 'speak comfortably to the people' (avoiding unpleasant subjects like death and hell); the beadle should be an earl's ex-butler; and the pew-openers, decayed governesses. Proprietary Chapels were often lucrative commercial ventures,[1] the vaults below being sometimes utilized as wine-cellars! In one well-known watering-place, tickets for seats were actually sold in public-houses (1852). 'I've heard of free churches,' *Punch* comments, 'but this ordering a pew with a pot of stout is free and easy indeed.'

It seemed strange that in a well-endowed church that claimed to be national, offering its services to the whole community, fees should be charged not only for pews, but for christening, marriage, and burials, etc. (*Punch's* displeasure was aroused in 1852 by the defacement of a memorial slab in Middlesbrough churchyard, not fully paid for). The Ecclesiastical Courts were 'little better than a den of thieves and a board of cannibals. In the Prerogative Court the fatherless and orphans are served up as the standing dish to clerks, registrars, and surrogates.'

More serious was the public sale of livings: 'Of all the blows that are aimed at the Church', said *Punch* in 1847, 'none are more likely to be injurious than those of the auctioneer's hammer.' Traffic in benefices was even worse than episcopal nepotism.

Flaunting advertisements extolled the size of the income, the convenience of the parsonage, the beauty of its grounds, and the social advantages of the neighbourhood, with the most casual reference to the souls for whom the 'incumbent' was to care. Auctioneers, vulture-like, reported on the

---

[1] There were honourable exceptions. That gifted Broad Churchman, Stopford Brooke, might never have secured a charge in the English Church had he not taken on Bedford [Proprietary] Chapel, London (cf. *Life*, by L. P. Jacks, 1917).

extreme age or delicate health of clergymen. The venerable rector of Shelfhanger (aged 90) complained of visitors who called to see how far his feet were in the grave! An advertisement of 1848 announces: 'The Patron of a Rectory of about £700 a year is desirous of presenting it . . . to a clergyman of not less than 80 years of age *of sound High Church principles*.' *Punch* suggested that the Patron should have advertised for 'a very old, old Warming-pan', as the young gentleman for whom the bed was destined would be leaving College in a very short time. Simoniacal practices ('Simple Simony')[1] abated by the eighties, thanks largely to *Punch's* spirited denunciation.

Other abuses were: the condition of London City churches, given over to decay and worship of Morpheus; the shockingly insanitary condition of churchyards ('Infection Glebe' rather than 'God's Acre'); and the right of the citizen to interment according to the rites of his own denomination. As Archbishop Tait complained, the last question 'threw the parochial clergy into paroxysms of wrath and alarm . . . one rector announced that he had provided pitchforks to repel the first Nonconformist funeral that should invade his churchyard'. Only after twenty years of heated controversy was this Anglican monopoly ended in 1881. Vested interests found no friend in *Punch*. Medieval educational and charitable trusts, under Church auspices, were often perverted under modern conditions, so that they failed to meet the needs of the poor, for whom they were originally intended. Thus the Master of St. Cross

---

[1] Mr. Duthie points out that 'a Buddhist, a Mohammedan, or even a declared Agnostic might present to a benefice, but not a virtuous or sincere Roman Catholic'. He cites an authentic case of a peer (Roman Catholic) advertising an advowson for sale: 'No Christian need apply.' 'And a Jew it was who became the owner of the right of presentation!' (*The Church in the Pages of 'Punch'*, pp. 172f.)

Hospital, Winchester, in 1848 a Peer in Holy Orders, received four-fifths of the revenues in return for looking after thirteen pensioners. *Punch* threw his influence against the sinecure holders. He also strove for a national system of education, such as Continental countries were then developing. 'No clerical interference!' was his watchword in 1850. 'Pay for your own schools!' Later, he grew aware of the dangers of secularism and favoured an 'agreed syllabus' that should provide Christian teaching in schools without ecclesiastical frills. Before the war of 1914, he was able to depict the lion and the lamb lying down together—the Bishop of London and that inveterate Nonconformist, Dr. Clifford, beaming on one another.

Punch had no sympathy with short-sighted ecclesiastics. To good Churchmen who wanted to retain the Athanasian Creed and yet had qualms over its damnatory clauses, he spoke frankly: 'If you don't believe it, say so.' He had no patience with the tenacious clericalism of those who sought to chain to the Holy Ministry Agnostics like J. A. Froude, who had long since ceased to be 'reverend'. (The Clerical Disabilities Bill, legalizing renunciation of Orders, introduced in 1862, did not become law till 1870.) *Punch* welcomed the Divorce Act of 1857: 'Whom the fiend had joined, God bless the hand that swift asunder smites.' He favoured cheaper divorce, and could see no moral bar to the few people who wanted to marry their 'deceased wife's sister'. Another kind of divorce that he favoured was the unnatural alliance of the Church and the liquor trade, by which subscriptions flowed into religious chests so long as Licences were unquestioned. On the other hand, *Punch* consistently refused to identify himself with the extreme Temperance party, for whom teetotalism was axiomatic and a measure to be enforced, if possible.

We have noticed that in its earlier day the London *Charivari* was strenuously progressive. That does not mean that the chronicle of national humour was on the side of the angels all the time. Erastian principle allowed that an endowed Protestant Establishment was indefensible in a country where Roman Catholics, mostly poor, constituted seven-eighths of the population. But when Convocation was restored in 1853 (it had 'lapsed into a state of innocuous desuetude' since 1717) *Punch* treated 'Parsons' Parliament' as a melancholy farce, instead of a step toward emancipation from the State yoke, a beginning in the art of spiritual self-government. *Punch* had an inveterate prejudice against Missions—all the more mysterious, since he expressed admiration for missionary heroes and hearty hatred of slavery (as in the Congo atrocities). He was probably wise in refusing to invoke the national arms to avenge the wrongs of missionaries. But he was cheap in his sneers about washerwomen round the Mission tub. On the lighter side, we are amused when his schoolboy explains to mother that the heading 'S.P.G.' in his diary does not mean 'Society for the Propagation of the Gospel', but 'Sundries, probably grub'!

Punch had no patience with Jewish Missions. 'The new grace is only given before meat!' In other words, he was sceptical about the genuineness of conversions, and in right Philistine style wanted to know the exact cost of every Hebrew turned Christian. Apart altogether from Missions, *Punch* was more unjust toward the Jews than any other race or faith. He merely continued the coarse Georgian tradition of depicting the 'sheeny' in an unpleasant light (like that other Victorian repository of humour, the 'Bon Gaultier Ballads').

Jewish Emancipation only came in 1858, and *Punch* (for once) was found in the company of political reactionaries and obscurantists. Thereafter, however, he made *amende honorable* for his previous injustice. Tenniel's famous drawing, censored in Russia, represented the Czar,

Alexander the Third, as the New Pharaoh oppressing the Chosen People (one of the few cartoons based on Scriptural themes).

Another of *Punch's* pet prejudices was a deep-seated suspicion of the Religious Orders that were being introduced, both Roman and Anglican. Monasteries and nunneries were to him sinister abodes of evil and misery. When a French monk made himself the *enfant terrible* of the Vatican and emulated Luther by taking a wife, he received a bouquet: 'Well done, Hyacinthe, my son!' The dogma of Papal infallibility provoked a much smaller schism of 'Old Catholics' than Protestants expected; but when French anti-clericals succeeded in disestablishing the Church in 1905 on the grounds that it was anti-republican, and interfered even with religious orders that nursed the sick, *Punch* interposed in the interests of equity. By the time Frederick Temple had become Archbishop of Canterbury (1896), a Roman Catholic editor sat in the editor's chair. 'No thoroughfare' is written up over many of the avenues of religious and theological thought 'into which his predecessors did not hesitate to walk with confident steps' (Duthie).

For the first fifty years of his life *Punch* was one hundred per cent Protestant,[1] a pronounced Low Churchman, an unrepentent Erastian, with a leaning to the Broad Churchmanship of Dean Stanley and F. D. Maurice. Kingsley, author of *Westward Ho!* (stalwart Protestant, 'muscular Christian', and friend of the under-dog), was his hero, though he could hardly congratulate him on the result of his controversy with Newman.

When it was rumoured that Mr. Gladstone was so 'High' that he had secretly become a Romanist, *Punch* ridiculed the idea (1871). He could not imagine the great

---

[1] But when Bishop Bickersteth refused to allow the inscription 'R.I.P.' on the tomb of a parishioner at Marsden, *Punch* protested against his narrowness ('The Bishop's Ban', 1875).

Liberal leader joining one of the most reactionary institutions in the world; but the national jester could not see eye to eye with a powerful unit of the Protestant army. This was the Evangelical party, which was much more influential in the Church of England than at the present day.[1]

The Evangelicals took life too seriously. In their puritanical rigidity, they forgot that even Faber the Romanist had the grace to sing 'that the love of God is broader than the measures of man's mind'. Amusements of all kinds, from the playhouse to cards and dancing, were strictly banned. The legalist prohibitions of parents often drove into 'the world' children whose liberty was unduly restricted. Novels, even poetry, were taboo. The *Record*, organ of Evangelical Anglicanism, in 1863 denounced *Good Words*, which the Rev. Norman McLeod of the Church of Scotland had founded as a means of bridging religion and life, by providing wholesome popular literature. To the *Record*, such a project was 'a union with Christ and Belial' —especially when heretics like Kingsley and Stanley were contributors. These furious articles were reprinted as pamphlets and circulated all over England and Scotland. One of the most fanatical opponents of amusements was Dean Close of Carlisle—incidentally an early pioneer of 'Prohibition'. The leading Rector of Salford would have no curate who smoked: *Punch* commented that he evidently did his own 'puffing'. Lord Shaftesbury's philanthropy was universally honoured by a grateful nation, ready to welcome practical Christianity. It was a pity, however, that his opinions were so rigid. When Seeley wrote one of the first modern studies of the ethics of Jesus (still a classic) his

[1] But Rev. D. W. Duthie is quite wrong in his assertion that the Evangelicals were ever 'a magnificent and proud majority'. Balleine, in his *History of the Evangelical Party in the Church of England* (1911 ed.), makes it clear they were always in a minority in the English Church.

C

Lordship denounced *Ecce Homo* as 'the most pestilential book ever vomited from the jaws of hell'. In 1850 *Punch* elevates him to the Peerage as 'Lord Sackcloth and Ashleys'. In the same number he is pilloried in an envelope for his opposition to the Sunday delivery of letters. In this instance 'the Evangelical of Evangelicals' was surely right in claiming a day of rest for the plodding postman. But *Punch* was right in objecting to extreme Sabbatarianism on the grounds that the Sunday closing of picture galleries and museums, etc., meant the filling of bars (he even branded Archbishop Tait, whom he generally admired, as 'the publican's best friend').

The Mecca of Evangelicalism in the early Victorian period was Exeter Hall, a rock of righteousness, past which roared the tide of worldliness in the Strand. 'Half conventicle, half concert room'—Exeter Hall was the headquarters of aggressive Evangelism. In the month of May particularly, you could hear missionaries fresh from darkest Africa, or listen to that remarkable colporteur, George Borrow (author of *The Bible in Spain*), denouncing the Romish Church, or sit at the feet of a celebrity like Pearsall Smith who declared that perfection was attainable even in this world. One recalls Charles Lamb's irony: 'I walked on a little in all the pride of an Evangelical peacock.' *Punch* had little use for pietistic cliques, with their 'holier-than-thou' attitudes and their sanctimonious 'language of Canaan' (cf. Trollope's Mr. Slope). There was doubtless a good side to Exeter Hall, as G. R. Balleine has pointed out in his *History of the Evangelical Party in the Church of England*. This historic place of meeting came to be used by speakers of all shades of opinion. Even the voice of Cardinal Manning was heard there in 1868. *Punch* considered it was 'all up with Exeter Hall'. With Dr. Cumming in mind—the orator whose pet obsession was 'the Number of the Beast in Revelation—he added, 'Let us no longer talk of Exeter Hall. Had we not better call it 666 Strand?'

Although *Punch* did not subscribe to the shibboleths of 'Evangelicalism', he (and many other Englishmen) maintained an uncompromisingly Protestant attitude toward the Reformed worship of the Church, threatened by 'Puseyism' and 'ritualism'. That innocuous prelate, Bishop Blomfield, he called 'Janus' because he insisted on the London clergy wearing the surplice in the pulpit, instead of leaving the reading-desk for the vestry, to emerge in the glory of gown and bands. It is a pity that the preacher's gown, customary in the English Church since the Reformation and a symbol of fellowship with the Lutheran and Presbyterian Churches, should gradually have been abandoned, even by Evangelicals, from the eighties onwards.[1] This was 'the thin end of the wedge'. The surplice not only appeared in the pulpit, but even invaded the choir—though for many years a feature of 'advanced' churches (cf. Samuel Butler's *Way of all Flesh* and Mrs. Oliphant's *Perpetual Curate*). The old-fashioned village choir in the back gallery, with its trombones and 'serpents', is brought to our affectionate remembrance when we read the novels of George Eliot and Thomas Hardy.

When *Punch* was young the Parish Clerk was still an important functionary. In country parishes at least, he was second only to the parson, giving out the notices and metrical psalms (hymns were only gradually coming in—an innovation smacking of Methodism). He further acted as the people's mouth-piece by repeating the responses in a loud voice and assisting at baptisms and weddings. His desk

[1] Canon Fleming, a well-known London preacher, thought that Evangelicals could strengthen their case against vestments, if they gave up the gown, for the use of which there was no legal sanction, only tradition. As regards the North of England, it is still worn in 15-20 parish churches.

was a conspicuous furnishing in every church, the outward
and visible emblem of his high office. But the Oxford
Movement, in alliance with less theological factors, combined to banish the venerable Parish Clerk. 'The chancel
would be re-quired, but he would not be required. Alas!
poor relic of a dull time, your distinguishing feature was
your "Amenity".' *Punch* did not waste sympathy on the
passing of the pew-opener, who automatically disappeared
with the removal of the old box pews. She was usually an
ill-favoured elderly woman with a bonnet and a palm
itching for a tip—*pro pu-dor* (pew door)! Listen to the
following conversation. *High Church Lady :* 'I suppose
that was the lady chapel behind the choir?' *Low Church
Verger :* 'I don't fancy there's hany such name 'ereabouts
m'm. I think it was only the pew-opener!' (1892). The
Verger, however, was to survive into the new era, and
Punch has never ceased to marvel at his psychological
make-up and his curious historical lore.

The first half of the nineteenth century was the closing
phase of Georgian neglect in the church fabric. St. Paul's
Cathedral was in a disgraceful condition in 1844. *Punch*
noted the uncleaned windows and grimy aisles, the perfunctory clergy and the scanty congregations; the unsightly
organ loft with pipes like superannuated gas fittings, block-
ing the entrance to the choir, locked up out of service time,
to the profit of the vergers. The Bishop's throne wanted a
leg, the wretched little pulpit had a sounding-board 'like a
crippled dumb-waiter'. The Communion Table was covered
with a tarnished cloth, a ragged carpet in front. 'The most
precious portions of the Communion Plate had been stolen
early in the nineteenth century; the emoluments of the
Chapter had not been used to replace the Eucharistic
vessels; so (they) were of the ugliest possible pattern and
of little intrinsic value.' Improvements were effected in
1871, but with reluctance.

Punch was a utilitarian in some respects—he could not appreciate the chiming of bells, for instance; but his judgement was certainly sound as regards the injudicious 'restoration' of churches, which was in full blast in his youth.[1] Many adherents of the Gothic Revival[2] were 'Goths' despite their pedantic veneration for the past. *Punch* quotes an advertisement:

> To be sold—Carved Oak Pulpit; handsome Stone Font, date unknown—curious oak panelling, time of Queen Elizabeth— all in consequence of the restoration of the Church.

> Brisk firewood prices were realized, and marine-store dealers seemed to be having what their American cousins call 'a good time'. Some of the decorators, probably members of Archaeological Societies, were heard to deplore the loss sustained through much of the old wood having been appropriated surreptitiously by the workmen for their own fires.

The Gothic Revival turned out a surprisingly large number of novels dealing with Church Restoration, one of them with the unattractive title, *Pews and Pewholders*.[3] The old-fashioned box pew was like a King Charles's head

---

[1] 'Church restoration' was the fashion among the gentry and clergy; the ordinary people were often opposed or indifferent. Coventry Patmore's verse gives a delightful picture of the movement that might easily have come straight from *Punch*:

> I rode to see
> The church—restorings; lounged awhile,
> And met the Dean; was asked to tea,
> And found their cousin, Frederick Graham,
> At Honor's side.

[2] *Punch* might have made much of that astounding Roman Catholic Convert, the Gothic Revivalist, A. W. Pugin (cf. M. Trappes-Lomax. *Pugin: A Medieval Victorian*, 1932).

[3] F. E. Paget, 1842. F. A. Paley's *Church Restorers* followed in 1844.

to the 'ecclesiologist'. Fr. Ignatius, the eccentric pioneer of revived monasticism in the Anglican Communion, went into a friend's church at Norwich one night with an axe, and by morning every box pew was laid low. The gradual disappearance of the squire's capacious enclosure deprived *Punch* of many openings for humour; one recalls how Mrs. Carlyle made for herself in one of them 'a sort of Persian couch out of the praying cushions and went to sleep'. *Punch* did not favour exclusiveness in God's House, but in 1856 derided the free chairs which ritualists considered adequately ecclesiastical.[1] Nevertheless, the pew survived in most churches (despite spartans who wanted bare, open benches). 'Soft cushions, easy backs, well-stuffed hassocks, and a fifteen-minutes' sermon' still appealed to those who wanted 'ease in Zion'. Not even these comforts were infallibly successful in attracting those who ought to set an example. A certain Vicar was reproaching his Squire for non-churchgoing. 'As a leading man in the parish, you ought to be one of the pillars.' The reply was more characteristic of 1945 than 1880. 'Well, at all events, if I'm not a pillar, I'm one o' the buttresses—always to be found outside, you know.'

---

[1] A praiseworthy Tractarian aim was to keep the church open on weekdays. As late as 1888 *Punch* reported, 'open churches are rare'.

III

MISS AMY CRUSE has reminded us that the sermon was a great institution in the Victorian era; indeed, most regular churchgoers felt that the minimum half-hour was stinted measure ('Preachers and their Hearers', Chapter 6, *The Victorians and their Books*, London, 1935). Stalwarts like Lord Balfour of Burleigh would go far to hear eminent preachers of every denomination, noting theological merits and method of delivery. Such eager seekers would 'go a Sabbath Day's journey and sit under them with the true ear of a hearer of the Word'.

Punch was too latitudinarian to sympathize with such zeal. He would have approved of Winifred Holtby's title for a book on the future of the pulpit (1928)—*Eutychus*. Readers will remember Acts 20:9: 'and as Paul was long preaching, he sunk down with sleep.' *Punch's* 'Eutychus Junior' asks: 'Why do they play the organ so loud for, when Church is over? Is it to wake us all up?' Every preacher tries to 'stab the spirit wide awake' when Morpheus is in the ascendant by arresting 'asides' as well as startling appeals. One country parson knew how to evoke a satisfactory response, the London *Charivari* reported in 1841: 'Oh, my brethren, avoid this practice (swearing), for it is a great sin, and what is more, it is ungenteel!' If the clergy persisted in preaching long dreary sermons[1] ('a clerical error'), a 'Patent Pulpit', furnished with a clock and mechanical Gothic canopy, might descend on the parson

[1] Benham's *Book of Quotations* quotes *Punch* (9th June 1877). ARCHITECT (who has come about the 'Restoration'): 'Good deal of dry-rot about here!' GARRULOUS PEW-OPENER: 'Oh, sir, it ain't nothink to what there is in the pulpit.' (Drawing by Keene.)

and painlessly extinguish him after he had preached long enough—an ingenious 'Early Closing' device.

Punch did not favour extempore preaching, however, as a sure means of keeping people awake. He thought every word ought to be well weighed before being uttered, and he mistrusted 'that dangerous facility given by active jaws and a hot imagination'. He believes in the written discourse—provided it is the preacher's own. He is dead against the trade in manuscript sermons (which still survives in the more plausible form of typescript). A man who is incompetent or too lazy to write his own sermons has no business in the pulpit. If he is hard pressed by other duties, he should publicly admit that it is borrowed. A famous London Canon preached *and published* a sermon on the wickedness of great cities; it bore a close resemblance to one of Dr. de Witt Talmage, the sensational pulpit orator of Brooklyn. This might appear a case of 'parallel inspiration' —but for the fact that lists of English cities were substituted for American ditto (see A. G. Gardiner, 'A Famous Sermon', *Leaves in the Wind*). 'Alas, for it was borrowed' (2 Kings 6₅). No doubt many another preacher has feared the accusation of plagiarism. Mark Twain, congratulating Bishop Doane on a sermon, observed that he had read every word of it in a book. The good bishop was greatly perturbed till he received a copy of the book in question—an English Dictionary!

Among the attractions of Victorian London were the great Nonconformist preachers. There was Spurgeon, holding forth to several thousands every Sabbath in the Metropolitan Tabernacle. Spurgeon was an institution, though many of his appreciative hearers (e.g. Ruskin) could hardly agree with his strong Baptist views and uncompromising Calvinism. *Punch* estimated that in every sermon he used no less than three tons of coals, all red hot. He did not care for his 'comic conventicle style', and for some years almost considered him a mountebank; but in course of time *Punch* appreciated Spurgeon at his true worth, vindicated his right to enjoy a cigar[1] (which some narrower co-religionists denied), and paid him a noble tribute at his death in 1892. Spurgeon, on his part, collected all the cartoons that burlesqued him; as a militant saint with a saving sense of humour, he valued them.

Another picturesque personality was Dr. Joseph Parker of the City Temple—individualistic, rhetorical, dramatic. *Punch* saw in him something of a Hebrew prophet, something of a showman, and something of a politician. Who could forget his daring New Year Admonitions to Queen Victoria and his melodramatic curse on the Sultan? *Punch* had no special desire to see Dr. Parker, or other 'eminent Nonconformist divines' appearing in Low Anglican pulpits. When 'inter-change of pulpits' was suggested by an Oxford Professor of Political Economy in 1868, the London *Charivari* poured cold water on the idea:

> Alack and alas, those Oxford codgers
> Have rejected erudite Thorold Rogers,
> > Because in zeal with error to grapple,
> > He dared to speak in a Baptist chapel,
> They'd rather live in total eclipse,
> Than be led to truth by the light of Dips.

When the *Morning Post* declared that no Dissenting preacher could hope for more advancement than a crowded chapel, a thousand a year, and endless invitations to five o'clock dinners, *Punch* thought that this destiny did not sound too bad; but he had no liking for Dissenters, whose

---

[1] One recalls Cowper's lines to Mr. Bull, a Congregational Minister, who combined the passion for souls with a love of tobacco:

> So may the smoke-consuming Bull
> Be always filling, never full.

extreme Evangelicalism and Puritanism were akin to the views of the Low Churchmen of Exeter Hall. He was unjust in accepting at its face value the caricature of a Nonconformist which had descended from the seventeenth century via Swift, Johnson, Sydney Smith, and Dickens. To Thackeray a chapel was 'a dingy tabernacle where a loud-voiced man is howling about hell fire in bad grammar'. One feels that *Punch* made little attempt to understand the best spirit of Dissent. His remarks on rural Nonconformity, however, are significant. There is the Methodist local preacher who falls out with his fellow sectarians and tells the Vicar his tale of woe: 'Yes, sir, after treatment the likes o' that, I says to 'em, "For the future," says I, "I chucks up all religion, and I goes to Church".' Then there is the rector's odd-job man who excuses himself for cutting the grass at the chapel by pleading that he doesn't use the same scythe.

'The Dissenter whose money becomes the reason of his apostasy from the faith of his father is especially abhorrent. Nor does he appreciate the tactics which permit a man to be a prominent Methodist in business and ostentatiously Anglican on his retirement to a brand new estate' (Duthie). While *Punch* attacks this snobbery, he does not attack one of the main causes—the fact that a privileged Church set on a social pinnacle since 1662 draws to itself the worldliness that does not find itself at home in the more democratic Free Churches. On the other hand, *Punch* realizes that during the Victorian period a considerable portion of the lower and middle classes had ranged themselves on the side of the Dissenters. So he declares against barriers of equal citizenship. While he laughs at the festive Oxford undergraduate who cuts his chapels by pretending he has become a Dissenter, he leads the agitation against University Tests, and when the academic gates swing open to men of every sect, his 'well done!' rings true.

Punch's chief aversion was the itinerant preacher. He pictures three lugubrious specimens in frock-coats 'holding forth' on Hampstead Heath, while a donkey-hirer surveys them with amused contempt. When Spurgeon admitted that dancing would be 'a profitable exercise', Leech depicts a company of godly men in huge white chokers grimly revolving round one another. Yet even the narrowest of sects, he realized, had their *raison d'être.* 'I'm very sorry to hear, Mrs. Brown,' said the Vicar, 'that you were present last night at a "Plymouth Brethren's" Tea Meeting. I have told you that these Doctrines are highly erroneous!' 'Erroneous, sir, their Doctrines may be; but their cake, with Sultany Raisins, is excellent!' Thackeray used to say that the best meal he ever ate was given him by a Quaker at Darlington. The quaint costume and scriptural speech of the Friends, which was not yet extinct, naturally excited good-natured banter. 'Now what are the peculiar distinctions of the Quakers?' Du Maurier's schoolboy is asked. 'For instance, how do they speak differently from you and me?' 'Please, sir, they don't swear!' In 1852 Leech depicted a Quaker relieving the British Lion of his gun, offering him an umbrella instead. There was more to be said for the 'umbrella' policy before the outbreak of the Crimean War than in 1938. John Bright and Cardinal Wiseman are seen embracing each other as allies in the unpopular anti-War cause. *Punch* respected the reserve, good breeding, and good citizenship of the Friends—and also of the Unitarians, another small body whose influence was out of all proportion to their membership; to Dr. Martineau, the leading intellect in the latter school of thought, he paid affectionate tribute on his ninetieth birthday. Till as late as 1898, when General Booth was caricatured as 'Bombastes Furioso', *Punch* was distinctly hostile to the Salvation Army; in spite of heroic social work, 'corybantic Christianity' was not appreciated. However, it is conceded that the housemaid who writes the Army's title in 'converted commas' is perfectly correct. Victorian employers were often concerned about the 'religious persuasion' of their servants. One Anglican spinster, exercised in soul on account of her domestic joining the Plymouth Brethren, asked: 'But, Rebecca, is your place of worship consecrated?'—'Oh, no, Miss, it's galvanized iron!'

Passing over Shakers, Mormons, and other 'fancy religions' for lack of space, we pass on to the Church of Scotland. In early Victorian times Dr. Guthrie travels on the Sabbath to preach against Sabbath travelling. Dr. Cumming, of Crown Court, London, in the middle of the century attracts hordes of Sassenachs, like Edward Irving, before him, as he unwraps the dark sayings of the Apocalypse, sets forth the signs of the times, and foretells the end of the world. When his predictions failed, he chose another date; this time he was 'positive'. This prophet of catastrophe nevertheless took his house on a fifty years' lease, and naïvely replied to *Punch's* amused protest that a belief in prophecy should not override common sense.

Dr. Cumming was certainly not a representative Scottish Minister; yet Scotland teemed with interesting personalities during the Victorian period. Instead of exploring genuine Scots humour, *Punch* evidently preferred the synthetic 'Scotch' joke, typified by the specimen in Benham's *Book of Quotations*. SOUTHERNER (*in Glasgow, to Friend*): 'By the way, do you know McScrew?' NORTHERNER: 'Ken McScrew? Oo, fine! A graund man, McScrew! Keeps the Sawbath, an' everything else he can lay his hands on.' (Drawing by Keene, 15th October, 1887.) Sly acquisitiveness, an insatiable appetite for Sermons, Sabbatarianism, and Scotch whisky are the main ingredients for concocting the religious humour of Caledonia.

It must be admitted, however, that the Kirk was ill served

by some of her own ministers of the 'Kailyard School', who followed Barrie's recipe for novels and sketches—drenched with sentiment and flavoured with 'pawky' humour. One thinks of Ian Maclaren and S. R. Crockett. To quote Hepburn Miller, the historian of Scottish literature: 'The circulating libraries became charged to overflowing with a crowd of ministers, precentors, and beadles, whose dry and "pithy" wit had plainly been recruited at the fountain-head of Dean Ramsay;[1] while the land was plangent with the sobs of grown men, vainly endeavouring to stifle their emotion by an elaborate affection of "peching" and "hoasting".' Occasionally *Punch's* humour is in quite an authentic vein, as when the beadle (magnifying his office) precedes the visiting preacher on the usual journey from the vestry to the pulpit, enjoining him to 'follow at a respectful distance'. A minister, back from holiday, asks: 'Well, Daniel, my good man, and how have things been going?' The beadle's reply is disconcerting—''Deed, Sir, a 'things been gaun on brawly. They say that you meenisters aye tak' guid care to send waur men than yoursel's to fill the poopit, but ye never dae that, Sir!' (1907). Another unexpected reply from a 'minister's man' is worth quoting. 'And so, Saunders, you think that we ministers ought to get larger stipends?'—'Aye. Ye see, we wad get a better class o' men!' (1908). This affords food for thought in our more socialistic era. Gunning King, who did the last two drawings, is obviously at home when depicting the kirk and its worthies.

The Victorian Scot was an unbending denominationalist. Keene introduces us to a staunch old lady, buying eggs in 1879. She complains about the price of butchers' meat. McTreacle the grocer suggests, 'You should turn a vegetarian'. 'A vegetarian! Na, na! Ah was born and brocht up i' the Free Kirk, an' A'm no gaun ta change ma

[1] *Reminiscences of Scottish Life and Character* (1857).

releegion!' According to *Punch*, the doughtiest supporters of the Free Kirk were elderly females with an inveterate suspicion of organs (which were being cautiously adopted during the seventies). Only occasionally do U.P.'s come into the picture. Two elders are seen coming out of their kirk, in all the glory of 'Sabbath blacks' and 'lum hat'. Says one: 'The meenister need'na been that haurd en hes discoorse. Theer planty o' leears i' Peebles, forbye me!'

Punch pictures an elder discussing with a friend a certain candidate's preaching in the kirk 'vacancy'. 'In my opeenion he wasna justified in dividing folk into the sheep and the goats. I wadna say, Jamie, that *I* was among the unco guid, and I wadna say that *you* were among the unco bad. So whaur do we come in? He'll no do for us, Jamie. We'll no vote for him.' The question of the election of ministers reminds us that the Disruption of the Church of Scotland occurred mainly because Parliament, predominantly English, had refused to abolish or modify lay patronage. Had *Punch*, along with other influential London papers, been alive to the seriousness of the situation in 1841, the Scottish Kirk might never have split in 1843. *Punch* was a righter of wrongs in those days, but unfortunately wore Erastian blinkers. Even today, the English mind does not comprehend Scotland and its Presbyterian Faith.

IV

'*PUNCH* IS no longer a theological expert,' observed the Rev. D. Wallace Duthie in 1912, 'the region of men's conscience is safe from him' (*The Church in the Pages of Punch*, p. 106). Roman Catholics, Anglo-Catholics, and others who strayed from Protestant orthodoxy had no further fear of his castigation or admonition. Critics might object that he had become a Gallio, who 'cared for none of these things'. As early as 1879 he represents a prospective curate giving a short and comprehensive answer to a Rector's question as to his 'views'. 'Well, Sir, I'm an Evangelical High Churchman of Liberal opinions.'

Certain it was that *Punch* was no longer the Reformer he had once been; like many elderly people, he had grown conservative. When the barriers of reaction were swept away by the Liberal victory of 1906, he did not share in this triumph. He had no sympathy with the upsurge of Nonconformist enthusiasm which made Puritanism count in the national life, as it had never counted since Cromwell. He was inclined to side with the upper classes in distrust of the mildly socialistic schemes of Mr. Lloyd George. He resented the way in which this little Welsh Baptist attorney mixed up religion and politics. 'When is a church not a church? When it's a tabernacle.' This definition may be illustrated from *A Land-Taxer's Diary* (21st August 1912). The Liberal candidate records: 'SUNDAY: Church in morning. Vicar read with undue emphasis the commandment about coveting neighbour's house or land—prostituting his pulpit to help a political party. Gave address in Baptist Chapel in afternoon. Subject: "Liberal Ethics." Very impressive when "Land Song" was sung after prayer. Think I stand a chance.' Another scene—'Blackfield's

Tabernacle' (19th June 1912).   A huge and enthusiastic
Nonconformist gathering is assembled to hear Silvester
Horne, Dr. Horton, Robertson Nicoll, etc.   Full-blooded
Radical oratory is going strong.   'We stand tonight, gentlemen, with Luther (cheers), with Knox (renewed cheers), as
representative martyrs of the human race.   We may be
sneered at by the lordly Cecils as they batten on their
monastic plunder (loud cheers), but a time will come when
our influence will control the government of this country!'

Sir Edward Carson enters and is given a tumultuous
welcome, but it is quite evident that the ultra-Protestant
of Ulster has little in common with the 'Passive Resisters'[1]
and Nonconformist Pacifists of 'Little England'.   The pro-
ceedings are eventually concluded by the Chairman (Dr.
Clifford) being presented by the Editor of the *Expositor*
with Foxe's *Booke of Martyrs* and a complete set of the
novels of that prolific Nonconformist, Silas K. Hocking
(194 volumes—'which will be read even when Caine is
forgotten').

Dr. Clifford, the very personification of 'Political Non-
conformity', announced at Westbourne Park Chapel,
London: 'I understand you have only one Welsh Saint.
Well, there'll soon be another; it will be St. Lloyd George.
I would canonize him right away.'   This *Punch* proceeds
to do by sketching him with a halo, golfing.

When Lloyd George opened his campaign against the
Welsh Church[2], he did not receive the support from *Punch*

---

[1] They were vocal in objecting to paying taxes for denomina-
tional schools.   'Their martyrdom was half-joyous excitement.
Had not *Punch* expressed the general feeling (well, anyhow, of the
classes that matter)? "Have you any cheap marters today?" Woman
at fruit-stall, looking round to see: "No, we're just out of passive
resisters."'   (E. Thompson, *John Arnison*, p. 267, London, 1939.)

[2] Not everyone understood the real issues.   Thus at the Guards
Club Doddles remarked: 'Disestablishing *welshers*—jolly good
thing for the Turf!'

that was so whole-heartedly accorded to Gladstone's Irish Disestablishment Bill. Nonconformity had too often transgressed the line separating politics and religion, and the 'Nonconformist Conscience' did not often keep in step with the likes and dislikes of the ruling class. *Punch* did not always realize that the Free Churches of England still had grievances, and that their one-sidedness was largely the result of a superiority-complex on the part of the State Church, aided by the party of privileged and vested interest.

Anglo-Catholic intolerance, however, found in the jester no supporter. He was on the side of good will in the Kikuyu controversy (1914) as in the Colenso case. How could 'the White Man's Burden' be sustained by missionaries at sixes and sevens? Well might natives sing their doleful lay, 'Why do de Christians rage?' That an Anglican colonial bishop could prevent the missionaries of his Church from engaging in inter-communion with non-episcopal missionaries seemed scandalous. So when *The Times* reported that Bishop Weston of Zanzibar had arrived in London, and had gone to the 'House of Charity', Greek Street, *Punch* remarked: 'And a very good address for him.'

The two years that preceded the first world war were ominous. Violence was the keynote. When the Welsh Bishops are held up by Highwayman McKenna, he blandly protests: 'Robbing you! Why, I'm letting you keep 12s. 6d. in the pound.' Strikes became so widespread that the *Almanack* for 1914 represented the clergy 'out' in goodly numbers to prevent a blackleg from taking a service! Suffragettes were to the fore in 1913, and there were several references to their misguided activity in the May number. One of the militant type, unable to light her fire for the tea-kettle, murmurs with annoyance: 'And to think that only yesterday I burnt two pavilions and a church!'

The stage was set for incendiarism on a biggar scale. But how strange the symbolism! The Kaiser, who was fond

D

of preaching in his own Lutheran churches, is pictured in a
surplice, standing at an eagle lectern, shells forming its
base—'Let us prey'! Three weeks later, he is portrayed as
THE GREAT GOTH: 'Design for a stained-glass window in a
neo-Gothic Cathedral at Potsdam.' His halo is fiery;
Malines smokes on his right, a dove flutters on his left. We
have almost forgotten that this War Lord had his apologists
even in the Church of England, which found German
Lutheranism 'wanting' in 'Apostolic Succession'. The
Archbishop of York resented 'the gross and vulgar way in
which the German Emperor has been treated in the news-
papers. . . . I have a personal memory of the Emperor very
sacred to me.' To which *Punch* retorted:

> His Grace of York maintains the Kaiser's
> Merely the dupe of bad advisers,
>   And simply to avoid a fuss,
>   Reluctantly made war on us.
>
> One marvels what his grace will say
> When, peradventure, some fine day,
>   Thanks to his German friends, he hears
>   York Minster crashing round his ears!
>   (2nd December 1914.)

Twenty years later a German agitator of Austrian birth,
a corporal in the first world war, was to make the Protestant
Church an integral part of the machinery of the Nationalist
Socialist State. On 24th October 1934 Adolf Hitler appears
in gown and bands, improving on Louis XIV: 'L'ÉGLISE,
C'EST MOI'!

In 1916 the Shakespeare Tercentenary Festival took
place about the same time as the four hundredth com-
memoration of the German Reformation. Martin Luther
greets Shakespeare thus: 'I see my countrymen claim you
as one of them. You may thank God you're not that. They

have made my Wittenberg—ay, and all Germany—to stink in my nostrils.'

It is a change to turn from these high themes to note the effect that the war had on ordinary Church circles in England. At a primitive seaside resort, an ancient mariner moralizes, with the parson as his attentive hearer: 'Ay, ay. This war has come on us for our vanity. Babylon fell for its vanity. And there never was as much vanity in Babylon as there was in Port Mugglesby last summer.' The younger generation needed instruction in the cause and cure of the war. An aged vicar addresses his Sunday-school. 'Now, children, we are to love our enemies. That isn't easy, is it?' SMALL BOY: 'No, sir.' VICAR: 'Well, how are we to do it?' (dead silence). 'Yes, we must love even the Germans,' continues the vicar, 'how are we to do that?' SMALL BOY: 'By giving 'em wot's good for 'em, sir!'

By September 1915 it was generally realized that the war was not going to be as short as many people expected. 'Our reserves' was now the watchword. A genial clergyman watches some street urchins armed with toy swords. 'But if you do not belong to the Royal Field Artillery, my boy, what is the meaning of R.F.A. on your shoulder?' 'Ready for anyfink, sir!'

The parson's daily round is, of course, affected by the war. When he calls on his parishioners, and inquires about the men abroad, he tries to quicken popular interest in the Bible, if they happen to be out East. 'These Salonikans, Mrs. Stubbs,' explained the vicar, 'are of course the Thessalonians to whom St. Paul wrote his celebrated letters.' MRS. STUBBS: 'Well, I 'ope 'e 'ad better luck with 'is than I 'ave. I sent my boy out three letters and two parcels, and I ain't got no answer to 'em yet.' Even in Church people are conscious of the background of war. 'Pick up the step there in the rear file!' orders the absent-minded colonel as the sidesmen march up to the altar with the offertory. The vicar's mind is so full of recruiting posters that he asks a bridegroom: 'Wilt thou take this woman . . . for three years or the duration of the War' (a limited contract that would have suited some Polish soldiers who took British wives in the second world war!). In any war a soldier's religion is of statistical importance to the authorities. One can understand the eager recruit, anxious to get into Kitchener's Army, on being asked his religion, replying in the most accommodating manner, 'Well, what are you short of?' A little more of that spirit would have neatly distributed the motley company of church-less men registered mechanically as 'Church of England'. Pathos and comedy mingle in the padre's announcement at a singsong: 'Lance-Corporal Gascoign, just in from the Somme, will sing: "A little bit of heaven."'

A fortnight after the Armistice the village parson looks in at the blacksmith's. 'And now, John, I suppose the time has come to beat our swords into ploughshares?' 'Well, I don't know, sir. Speaking as a blacksmith of forty-five years' experience, I may tell you it can't be done.' However uncertain the prospect of permanent peace, the changeover from war is set in action. Demobilization is the order of the day. On 8th January 1919 the parson greets a parishioner: 'I hear your husband is home from France. Is the Army going to release him?' 'Well, 'e's got a fortnight before he goes back, but by that time 'e hopes to be demoralized.'

The post-war period was certainly a time of demoralization as well as demobilization. Housing, unemployment, and all kinds of problems created by the war clamoured for solution. But now that the war was over, the idealistic slogans were laid aside, and the Geddes Axe was applied to the tree of reconstruction schemes. Agriculture, fisheries, and shipbuilding received little encouragement from the government. Only the plutocrat flourished. *Punch* tells

how the wife of a certain profiteer consulted her vicar about
the christening of her eighth child. 'And what do you
intend calling the little fellow?' 'Well, you see, my
'usband 'an me 'ave been thinkin' it over; an' seein' as 'ow
last year—the seventh since the war started, an' the time
things begun to look up for us—we called that one "Septi-
mus", we think this one's name should be "Octopus"'
(1922). And a very appropriate name for a baby profiteer!
No wonder that the Labour Party increased its membership. 'Going to the labour protest meeting?' the vicar asked
his gardener. 'Now, tell me, Reuben, what *are* your
grievances?' 'Woy, zur, that be just wot Oi be a-goin' fer
tew find out.'

There were, indeed, many innovations to disturb the
traditional ways of the countryside—the minister, 'spankin'
aboot on yon cyclopeady', heralded the advent of bus,
cinema, and wireless. Even in the earlier days of the
war 'picture houses' had multiplied in the larger towns.
Punch was amused at the 'candour' of a well-known
cricketing parson, the Rev. F. H. Gillingham, who
reported to the *Weekly Dispatch* in 1916: 'To satisfy
my mind I spent over two hours in a certain cinema.
. . . . Frankly, I was disappointed. I saw nothing
which could be in any way called indecent.' As far back as
1914, however, the trouble of juvenile delinquency could
be partly traced to the movies. In that year a distressed
mother dragged her offspring (dressed in 'Wild West' togs)
to the visiting clergyman. ' 'E's been an orful trial to me
ever since them pitcher palaces began. First 'e was shootin'
at the fowls, an' now 'e's pinchin' my woolly mats ter put
on 'is legs.' Contact with Americans during the war, combined with the popularity of ragtime and jazz, not to speak
of the 'movies' and later the 'talkies', gave American slang
a vogue which reached even the upper classes. Since the
war, the United States was more than ever the land of the

Almighty Dollar.[1] Transatlantic tourists poured into England. Impoverished English gentry were less averse to inter-marriage with wealthy Americans than in the easy pre-war days. 'Howdy, bo?' is the salutation with which the Lady of the Manor greets the astonished parson when he calls; 'I sure hope you're feeling full of pep? Excuse me, vicar, but I'm practising a few phrases so that in case I meet any of this American invasion I can make them feel at home.' The names of movie stars were becoming familiar even to the clergy. Thus a hostess at a dinner party, at a loss for a topic, asks a parson: 'Did you ever see "Charley's Aunt"?' 'Well, really, I'm ashamed to say, I've never seen even Mr. Chaplin himself.' According to Mr. Benet Finck, the 'naughty person' of Proverbs 6₁₃ is Charlie Chaplin: 'He winketh with his eyes, he speaketh with his feet' (*The Spreading Chestnut Tree*, London, 1945).

The coming of wireless did not help churchgoing, which had fallen on evil days. However, the B.B.C. tried to give with one hand what it had taken away with the other. 'Religious Services' were to be broadcast from churches as well as from the studio.[2] One vicar in August 1922 proudly

[1] Wonder was expressed at the excellence of the new American Architecture and the speed of building, compared to our own slow tempo. *Punch* visualizes the design for a magnificent neo-Gothic metropolitan church—acclaimed by the building committee and finished to the last detail in record time; but in a few weeks . . . skyscrapers have sprung up on all sides and dwarfed it to insignificance (Summer number, 1931).

[2] Before 1914 a monster gramophone in St. Mary's-at-Hill, London, reproduced 'in a husky bellow' the milder tones of his Grace of Canterbury.

> No longer need a curate rude
> dish up his weekly platitude,

observed *Punch*.

> So since for preaching, by your aid,   But one thing's left for you to do—
> The cream of sermons is purveyed,   Invent some scheme by which I, too,
> Of first rate orthodoxy,   Can go to church by proxy.

waited for the great congregation that was to inaugurate
this innovation in his own church. But as the time wore
on, an anxious look came over his face. 'This is terrible!
Five minutes before the service, and not a soul here!'
'No, sir,' replies the verger smoothly, 'but I understand
there are some thousands waiting in their own homes to
"listen in".' By 1935 broadcasting had developed to such
an extent that choral music had an assured place. So we
hear a verger tip-toeing to a worshipper in church and
whispering: 'The organist says would you mind not singing
so loud, sir, as we're broadcasting this service and you're
messing up the balance of the choir.' Most people are so
radio-conscious that they would quite understand the layman who was asked to read the Lessons in Church and
absent-mindedly concluded: 'That is the end of the Second
News.' To the aged and infirm, wireless worship has been
a blessing and a boon. On the other hand, the lazy and the
cantankerous find 'listening in' a cheap and easy substitute
for the House of God. (I recall the authentic case of a lady,
who, after falling out with every minister in a small town,
declared she had now joined 'the great Church of Unseen
Believers'!) The majority of English people have ceased
to be active members of any denomination—which results
in the Established Church being responsible for the pastoral
care of a useless roll of passive adherents. Vicar (1944):
'Well, John, do you go to church or chapel?' 'Well, sir,
if you asks me what I stops away from, it's church.' As
early as 1913 the same mentality was revealed in *Punch's*
loafer who replied to an interrogator: 'I canna richtly be
said tae gang tae any kirk, but it's the Auld Kirk I stay away
frae.' Even in Scotland this type of 'Christian' increases.

The two religious personalities who were most in the
public eye between the two wars were probably 'Dick
Sheppard' and 'the gloomy Dean'. Under H. R. L. Sheppard St. Martin-in-the-Fields became the nearest approach

to 'the parish church of the British Empire'. The devotion
and humanity of the vicar won him the affection of the
plain man everywhere, and to a unique pastoral instinct he
added a gift for straightforward public utterance. He was
all for a more democratic, inclusive Church, a juster social
order, a last crusade against war. Alas! *The Impatience of a
Parson* did little to advance the good causes he led so
bravely. *Punch* paid Dick Sheppard affectionate tribute during
his illness and represents him appropriately in a soft collar,
as the kind of parson that does appeal to many of the laity.

> To stronger hands the stricken shepherd yields
> The flock he folded in St. Martin's Fields;
> Gentle at heart to others' need and pain,
> May RICHARD shortly be himself again.

A Broad Churchman in theology, Dean Inge was an
unrepentant Conservative in politics. The Kingdom of God,
as preached by certain fellow-Churchmen, appeared to him
mere socialist propaganda. The vision of Christian Reunion
was 'a dream, and not even a pleasant dream'. Labels, of
course, are often libels. Inge was not entirely the Gloomy
Dean, as *Punch* points out—yet when we look back on that
dismal epoch between the wars, had he not good reason for
pessimism?

> How wisely he conciliates
> With sparkling essays in the Press,
> The Mammon of Unrighteousness;
> So that in case some rainy day,
> The pillars of St. Paul's give way,
> His occupation being gone
> *The Morning Post* may take him on.—(1926.)

After 'Munich 1938' *Punch* turned to the lighter side of
the crisis. An aged, white-tied vicar, meeting a female
parishioner, murmurs: 'Well, I shall never see us so near
war again.' To which the villager replies: 'Oh, vicar, don't

IN THE VESTRY

MINISTER (*who has exchanged pulpits—to Minister's Man*). 'Do you come back for me after taking up the books?'

MINISTER'S MAN. 'Ou ay, sir, I comes back for ye, and ye follows me at a respectful distance!'

say that!' Yet the storm broke out a year later. *Punch*
does not provide us with as much material on the second
world war as on the first, from the ecclesiastical point of
view[1] (the Church counted for much less than it did in the
former struggle). Two of his cartoons may be compared to
advantage. On 21st February 1923 *Punch* commemorates
Wren (1723–1923) by picturing the Bishop of London,
armed with a pickaxe, surveying the statue of the great
architect. 'Ah, Wren! Great man! what can we do to
honour his bi-centenary? I know. Knock some of his
churches down!' This 'HAPPY THOUGHT' was fulfilled in an
unexpected way by the Germans less than twenty years
later. On 3rd December 1941 we see an elderly couple
inspecting St. Paul's Cathedral, exposed to full view by the
demolition of surrounding buildings during the Blitz. The
wife explains: 'Actually, this is now very much as Wren
INTENDED to see St. Paul's.' In 1943 two officers are being
shown over an abbey ('Admission 6*d*.') ruined centuries
ago. 'Thanks to Mr. Higgins', said the Guide, 'it came
through the Blitz undamaged' (Higgins being a bearded
patriarch wearing a tin hat.) Before leaving ecclesiastical
antiquities it is relevant to remark that there must have
been consternation among vergers, guides, and local anti-
quaries, if they turned up *Punch* in 1940 to find Cromwell,
the destroyer of sacred shrines, extolled as a national hero,
inspiring Britain with his call for a united front. A new
'Ironside', however, the Lord soon raised up. In publicists'
lists of 'the world's greatest men' (*Punch*, 24th January
1912) the Kaiser ranked 9th, the Rev. Silvester Horne 12th,
and Winston Churchill 13th. Thirty years later the Man
who was only 13th was to top the class.

[1] Church parades are a perennial source of humour (to those
who are not affected). The following notice is authentic:
    'Roman Catholics will parade at 09.30, Church of England
at 09.45, and all other demons at 10.00 hours.'

V

LOOKING BACK to the beginning of the twentieth century, what kind of a picture do we get of the Church in action? We catch occasional glimpses of the Irish priest among his flock, and the Scottish minister with his parishioners. But *Punch's* detachment from his older polemical attitude, while admirable oecumenically, narrows his scope somewhat. As far as Scotland is concerned, much genuine humour *could* be collected from varied sources— Church Vacancy Committees, Sessions, Presbyteries, and not least the august General Assembly. But it is easier, of course, to collect a few stale 'chestnuts' of Cockney humour and serve them up to the public every now and again. On the other hand, one admits that occasionally *Punch* makes a shrewd hit. A lady, 'doing' the Scottish cathedrals, turns to her companion—'This is GOTHIC, isn't it, John?' A young girl in a straw hat (juvenile vendor of *Guides*) butts in. 'No, Mem. *THIS IS PRESBYTERIAN.*' Opposition to the reading of sermons and prayers is by no means dead north of the Tweed. However, even the preacher who is a 'reader' has his loyal supporters. 'The new meenister gave us a gran' sermon this mornin',' said one woman to another. 'Och, aye,' admitted her neighbour, 'it was awfu' fine. But d'ye ken he *read* it?' 'Read it! I wouldna' a' cared if he had *whustled* it!' (1919.) The minister's wife, the manse maid (*rara avis*), and the members of the Women's Guild would afford a fertile source of humour.

---

[1] The terror-producing sermons of Jonathan Edwards, delivered during the 'Great Awakening', 200 years ago, were *read*. As the preacher dilated on 'Sinners in the Hands of an Angry God', his only gesture was to turn the pages of his MS. This deliberate action added to the effect of his sermons.

Perhaps, however, it is asking too much of any London periodical to understand the kirk and its spirit. One might expect to find, then, a fair understanding of English Religion. *Punch* almost assumes that the Church of England is the sole representative of English religion. Nearly half the diminishing worshippers of South Britain are 'Free Churchmen' (a title, incidentally, they have 'pinched' from Scotland). Yet they are ignored by *Punch* (perhaps because most of his readers presumably attend either the parish church or the golf course on Sunday, and are too genteel to be aware of the existence of the Nonconformist chapel). Now that the heyday of 'political dissent' has long passed, no sound Conservative reader should object to denominations that are thoroughly English in temperament and ideals (unlike the advanced ritualist section of the National Church who have 'gone Italian' for years past, despite the ordered protest of 'Central Churchmanship'). Nor need those who cater for lawful amusement fear that 'the Nonconformist Conscience' will taboo all pleasure; ultra-Puritanism within the Free Churches seems to be on the decline, as regards cards, dancing, and the theatre. Nonconformity is no longer 'isolated from the main stream of national life', as Matthew Arnold used to say. Even before 1914 the popularity of pageants reached the non-Anglican Churches; *Punch* once met a broadminded deacon, who 'didn't mind being an Ancient Bishop in the cause of Charity !'

Punch has an effective 'presentation feature' (1st July 1914). Two ladies are being shown a carpet by a salesman. 'We're giving our pastor a new drawing-room carpet on the occasion of his jubilee. Show us something that looks nice, but isn't too expensive.' 'Here is the very thing, madam—real Kidder*minister*.' I suppose that in every denomination there is a type of plausible church worker who tries to 'kid 'er minister'! Then there are humorous openings that might be taken advantage of in the 'cock-and-en' choir, opportunities non-existent in the boy-and-man choir of the Anglican. In 1939 *Punch* referred to a Methodist minister's announcement at the close of a sermon which taxed the mental capacity of his hearers: 'The words of the anthem are: "Some day we'll understand, Some day we'll understand."' One would imagine that the Nonconformist minister and his wife would give the readers of *Punch* a change from the rector and his family. The 'flitting' to which most Methodist ministerial households are subject, every three years, would be a further source of humour(?).

The ministers of the Free Churches are still primarily preachers. That is suggested by the weekly advertisements outside their chapels: 'REV. X.Y.Z WILL PREACH HERE ON SUNDAY' (or sometimes one reads the alarming phrase, 'ALL DAY'). It is reassuring to see a 'Wayside Pulpit' bulletin immediately below, which may contain the motto: 'DON'T WORRY, IT MAY NEVER HAPPEN.' Free Churches have often been handicapped by well-meant but flamboyant publicity[1] which does their cause no more good than cheap-and-nasty 'Gothic' façades. Anglicans cannot teach everything, but can at least teach reverence and good taste. Anything that suggests 'religious vaudeville' of the base type (still flourishing in certain quarters in the United States) should be utterly banned. *Punch* reported on 2nd July 1913: 'Mr. Harry Lauder preached last week at the Castle Green Congregational Church, Bristol. He appears to have been the greatest success, and we can picture the sacred edifice ringing again and again with merry laughter.'

The rivalry of competing 'pulpit stars' is a discreditable

---

[1] *Punch* has recently found the following gem in a Glasgow paper.

AGENDA

.30.   Rev. Ralph Wynne Fairway.   Commences a new Ministry to Preach the Gospel, Reseat the Church, Redecorate the Interior, Modernize the Lighting, Overhaul the Organ, etc.

phenomenon of popular Protestantism on both sides of the Atlantic, and some 'religious weeklies' have sometimes fanned their favourites with publicity, so that this puffing tendency has been positively encouraged. From the days of Whitefield to Joseph Parker, preacher-worship flourished and the cult is by no means extinct; each coterie has its favourite pulpiteer and libations of adulation are liberally offered (and sometimes mysteriously withheld, for no apparent reason). The popular preacher of today can *promise*, but cannot *threaten* like his predecessor, who had a good command of 'the rich vocabulary of ecclesiastical vituperation', besides the effective argument of hell.[1] 'We are too polite in the pulpit,' said the Bishop of Chelmsford in 1923. This text suggested to *Punch* a tale of two preachers. We are not told their denomination, but colouring indicates that they belong to the Free Churches, one of them being obviously an adventurer from across the Border.

> Antoninus Brown
> Would always preach with eyes cast down
> Except when he forgot to;
> He used to speak of God as 'Gade',
> And never called a spade a spade
> (He thought it better not to).
> In short his manners were so kind
> That spinsters thought him 'most refined'.
>
> McCrusoe, on the other hand,
> Was almost anything but bland.
> . . . His speech was rough, his hair unkempt,
> He never hid the fierce contempt
> With which his flock inspired him.

[1] Modern congregations, but for convention, might leave the preacher 'alone in his glory'. *Punch* represents a near-sighted vicar preaching to pews all vacated. The verger tip-toes up the pulpit steps, with the keys. 'Do you mind locking up when you've done, sir?' (This story also circulates in America.)

> He spoke of them in scornful terms
> And called them 'Meeserable worms'.

Strange to relate, 'McCrusoe's church held half the town'. Brown therefore slipped into his rival's church and took note. He decided 'to go one better'. So he went in search of bad language.[1] He haunted Billingsgate. He frequented the company of bargees. Habitually he 'paid taxi-men their *legal* fare'. He then hardened his heart and preached. From Golders Green to Camden Town, he soon became the fashion. 'Some even left their Sunday games, to hear him call them nasty names.' His fame soon excelled McCrusoe's ('whose repertoire, though pretty tough, was hardly versatile enough').

> So, Preacher, if your church you'd fill,
> And make your congregation thrill,
>   Pray be a little bolder;
> Your party manners please forget,
> And do not be afraid to let
>   Us have it from the shoulder;
> For after all the Bishop's right—
> It's *no* use being *too* polite!

> (30th May 1923.)

The task of preaching and the wearing of a regulation uniform is common to Roman Catholic priests, Anglican clergymen, and most Protestant ministers. Fashions in clothes as well as in sermons have changed during *Punch's*

[1] Strong language, according to *Punch* (and many laymen), is the pet aversion of 'the cloth'. 'Can I help you?' a parson asks some men dealing with restive horses. 'Well, sir, if you wouldn't mind going a bit up the street, the horses will understand the language better.'
In 1919 a short-sighted traveller asks at the station: 'Is there some delay on the line, my good man?' NAVAL OFFICER: 'Who the —— do you think I am, sir?' S.T.: 'Er—n—not the vicar, anyway!'

eventful century. The neck-cloth was followed by the white tie. Various experiments in starched collars resulted in the complete triumph of the 'Roman Collar'. Originally the badge of the uncompromising Papist, it invaded the Anglican fold, then the Presbyterian,[1] and English Free Church strongholds. A correspondent in the *Church Times* a few years ago complained that it had lost all Churchly significance; one could not even be sure that it encircled a Christian neck, for Unitarian ministers and even Jewish rabbis had adopted it (some curious misunderstandings might result in amusing railway-carriage conversations!). Only Continental and American Protestantism seems to have fought shy of 'the collar'—citizens of the United States having a tendency to laugh at the custom of 'wearing one's collar the wrong way round' as peculiarly British. Nevertheless, clergy who arrive in canonicals at New York are said to have preferential treatment at the hands of Customs officials, who, being largely Irish as a personnel, mistake them for Catholic priests. But the clerical collar is not a universal passport to politeness—not in the East, anyway. 'You suspect *hashish*?' exclaimed a scandalized and correctly attired vicar on a Mediterranean cruise. 'But, good heavens, man, look at my collar!' To which the zealous Customs officer in his tarboosh retorted testily: 'Yess—Yess—plenty time. I search you under the collar in a minute' (*Punch*, 1932). As a symbol of respectability a clerical collar is a useful disguise provided the manners of the man who assumes it are in keeping. 'To don, or not to don?' is a living issue when burglars break into the parsonage.

Punch pictures FIRST CROOK surveying SECOND CROOK attired in borrowed canonicals. 'Well, it's a good effort,

---

[1] Fifty years ago Scotland (like Caesar's Gaul) was divided into three parts—ecclesiastically. You could usually tell by the style of his collar at a glance whether a minister was Established, Free, or U.P.

Nobby, but you'll be lucky if you get away with it.' It is not often that a wolf takes the risk of trying shepherd's clothing. But the 'dog-collar', like the 'wideawake' hat and the 'surtout', have undergone much ridicule since 1919. To certain laymen they suggest a 'holier-than-thou' attitude on the part of the clergy. There is nothing new in the objection to clerical attire on the part of young ministers. When R. F. Horton was at Oxford in the eighties and decided to become a Congregational pastor, he declined the title of 'Reverend' and declared: 'I shall wear no clothes to distinguish me from my fellow-Christians.' Whereupon an Oxford caricaturist pictured Horton, soaring in the skies and tearing off his clothes, piece by piece. Whatever may be said for clergy who prefer to dress like other professional men (and they have a case) the fact remains that Methodist ministers of the ex-Wesleyan tradition make a point of wearing the clerical collar, and yet they are said to be more in touch with the ordinary working man than parsons of any other Communion. Perhaps *Punch* may suggest some new line in 'shepherd's clothing'? Till then, most of us will have to put up with the despised 'dog-collar'. Sartorially speaking, it has surely important symbolic value in these days of active Christian co-operation—the clergy of all denominations can present 'a united front' to the world!

The Anglican prelate is no longer the 'ornamental bishop' of Victorian times, but still wears the apron. Soon after the last war a child asked: 'Is that a Highlander in mourning, mummy?' Apron strings symbolize the subjection of youth. In 1914 a bishop is represented with his back to a drawing-room fire. 'I can't think of letting you two girls go alone,' says a vigilant aunt, 'and as I shall not be able to go, your uncle will look after you.' NIECE: 'That's very kind of him, Auntie; but I hope you don't expect us to cling to his apron strings all the time.' About the same time *Punch* noticed *A Review of the Primates*, by

E

D. G. Elliot. The *Times Literary Supplement* had observed, *re* this learned work, that 'Monkeys, and especially the higher apes, have an unfailing interest for mankind'. *Punch* objects: 'But this is not the way that we ourselves should begin an article on the Archbishops.' The spirit of the age hardly cultivated reverence for even Church dignitaries. 'Can you tell me where the Dean hangs out?' asks a young man in 1936. 'The Dean doesn't 'ang out, sir,' replies a policeman, 'he *resoides*'. Even the clergy are sometimes incapable of calling correctly. 'Is the Bean dizzy?' inquires a clerical 'Spoonerist'[1] (1920).

Wars and revolutions change the face of the earth, but the English country clergyman goes on his rounds as usual. He is usually genial and well meaning, but does not always bridge the cultural gulf between himself and his rural parishioners as successfully as he thinks. Thus he asks a road-worker: 'Not emulating Sisyphus, I hope?' 'No, sir, I be shoving this blasted tar-barrel up the hill.' Even when he uses plain English, he is not always understood. An old wife murmurs to her husband coming out of church: 'Parson 'e be always askin' for money for 'is new 'eating apparatus'. Why don't 'e just say, as 'ow 'e wants a new set o' teeth?' Plain speaking is not always taken at its face value, as appears from the following dialogue: 'Good afternoon, Mrs. Gubbins. I was glad to see you in church. How did you like my sermon?' 'Well, sir, as I says as we was coming out, if you do talk plain and straight like in them sermons, there's the comfort of knowin' you don't mean 'alf you says, so we don't take no offence like, sir.' The villagers misunderstand others besides the parson,

[1] Whether the name of Dr. Spooner is known across the Atlantic is hard to say, but 'Spoonerisms' certainly are. 'Is it kisstomary to cuss the bride?' asks a nervous bridegroom. The clergyman replied, 'Not yet, but soon.' (*World's Best Jokes*, ed. Copeland, Halcyon House, New York, 1936.)

however. 'Dear me,' says the new vicar to a bedridden woman, 'And so you've kept your bed for three years'. 'Yes, sir, the doctor came three years ago and told me not to get up till he see me again, and I've never seen un since.'

The modern clergy seldom hunt or shoot, but they have their due share of recreation. A rector, who went on a world-cruise in 1924, had to rebuke an inebriate on his own return. The old reprobate replied: 'Well, sir, I can't afford to travel roun' the world, so mus' make world travel roun' me.' (*Punch* is rather too addicted to this type of joke.) One wonders how clerical temper is improved on the golf course—said to be a fertile field for the production of strong language. A golfing parson was putting badly in 1939. Was he concentrating on the ball? 'Ah! that was lack of consecration,' moralizes the bearded caddy. Many a clergyman must have spent his war-time leisure trying to amuse evacuees. This is foreshadowed in 1912 when a rural vicar has exhausted himself in the effort to interest 'London guttersnipes' in country scenes. Finally, he suggests a game of cricket. CHORUS: 'Why, mister, you ain't got no blooming lamp-post.' That reminds us of the type of minister who goes up to Town only to hunt books. 'These fine old theological works don't appear to be a very saleable commodity with you, my man,' says a keen book-hunter to the proprietor of a second-hand bookstall. 'Well, sir, the way is, we buys the books in lots, an' we 'as to take the bad with the good !'.

In these democratic days the clergy do not find that their office-bearers are all 'yes-men'. One vicar was having great difficulty with a tiresome individual at a parish business meeting. 'Really, Mr. Dash, are you the vicar or am I?' 'Oh, no, sir, I'm not the vicar.' 'Very well then, don't talk like an idiot.' Sometimes the social side of Church life is a relief to ministers who are 'good mixers'. 'All enjoying yourselves? That's splendid!' exclaims the vicar as he looks in at a whist drive in the parish hall (the harassed faces are too

E*

intent on 'pleasure' to notice him). Bazaars are mentioned by *Punch* as a new outlet for feminine enthusiasm in 1907. Years later, a curate greets his unfailing supporter (an unattractive looking specimen): 'Oh, Miss Tootsby, it's good to see you here again. It wouldn't seem like a jumble sale without you!'

It seems to be axiomatic in certain quarters that if an excursion is 'mixed' its success will be assured. But *that* does not always follow. 'We shall assemble at half-past nine,' said the vicar, announcing the annual 'outing' of the Mothers' Meeting, 'and—er—you may bring your husbands.' CHORUS OF MOTHERS: 'Oh, but we want to enjoy ourselves!' (1912.) We hear a variation of this theme in 1922, as we listen to a verger explaining to a visitor: 'That wasn't our parson preaching this morning. He be up in Lunnon. They've sort of exchanged dooties for a month.' VISITOR: 'A nice change for each of them.' The verger did not quite agree that this would mean unalloyed pleasure. He observed: 'They've both got their missuses with 'em.'

The lady of the parsonage has little leisure as a rule; her world is her husband's parish. Only occasionally is she 'contacted' by the politician. 'I say, Rector,' calls a Candidate from his car, 'I do wish you'd talk to your wife. I hear she's one of the doubtful women.' The Rector is properly shocked, not realizing that electioneers classify voters as 'O.K., DEAD, AND DOUBTFUL'!

The old-fashioned English gentleman is a thorough conservative. He does not understand the average modern clergyman, who is no judge of wine like many of his predecessors. He is astounded when he offers the new incumbent a glass of his very old port and is thanked thus: 'Most refreshing,' remarks this non-connoisseur—as though he had just swallowed a glass of lemonade! Nor does the invalid sporting squire exactly hit it off with the well-meaning curate (probably a townsman). 'Think of it, man, I've had no shooting, and I haven't killed a fish. . . . It's dreadful to be stuck indoors.' The nervous curate tries to be as sympathetic as he can: 'Quite—and of course there's so little one can *kill* indoors.' Nervousness in curates must make weddings an ordeal—especially when one of the contracting parties is deaf. CURATE (*forte*): ' . . . to have and to hold.' BRIDEGROOM: 'Eh?' CURATE (*fortissimo*): '*To-have-and-to-hold*.' BRIDEGROOM: 'To 'ave and to 'old.' CURATE: '*From-this-day-forward*.' BRIDEGROOM: 'Till this day fortnight!' *Punch* finds weddings a fertile field for humour. Gone are the days when he used to tilt at the fee-grabbing clergy. His sympathies are now with 'the cloth'. ' 'Ow much?' asks the Best Man curtly. 'Well, the law allows me seven and six,' replies the parson modestly. 'Then 'ere's 'arf-a-crahn; that makes it up to 'arf-a-quid.' We are not told whether the parson pointed out that the phrase 'the law allows' does not mean 'the law pays me'. It is usually the social side of weddings that attracts most attention. The verger's manner is most professional when approached about the details: 'Let's see, miss' (taking notes), 'there's bells you want, and awnin', and red carpet. Now what about choir-boys—they comes out at eightpence a-piece. Shall we say a dozen?' Funerals are of course not so much in *Punch's* line; he rather likes them to be 'Scotch' (no reference to the beverage once so intimately associated with the rite of burial!). 'And what for are ye wearin' yer blacks the day, Mr. McTavish?' asks a Scotswoman. 'I was at the Bailie's funeral.' ' 'Twill ha' been a gran' procession, likely?' 'Aye, but verra little enthusiasm.' (1922.) There are fashions even in funerals, and new methods worth considering. Two elderly ladies approach their clergyman: 'We have called, really, vicar, to ask your advice. My sister and I think of trying cremation.' (1933.)

The Church teaches that the body must be disciplined before it is finally committed to the elements from which it came. Ever since the Oxford Movement, the Anglican clergy have emphasized fasting in Lent. *Punch* used to ridicule the practice, and can still see its humorous side. MAID (waiting at table in Lent): 'Will you take a chop, miss, or have what the fast ones are takin'?' Does 'austerity' improve temper? 'My husband gave up smoking for Lent, you know.' GENTLEMAN: 'Splendid! And you, dear lady?' 'Well, I've been living in the same house with him.' One recalls Quiller-Couch's satire of parsonical personification to make the Church Year brighter. 'My brethren, as we feast and revel, catering for the inner man, Septuagesima creeps up to our elbow, and plucking us by the sleeve, whispers, "Lent is near"!' *Punch* would have little respect for 'that minatory virgin, Septuagesima'. Indeed, he is more interested in Harvest Thanksgiving services than in Lenten fasts. The display of fruit, vegetables, etc., appeals to the 'inner man' (especially in the age of rationing). 'Vicar looks rather well in his allotment,' is the stage-whispered comment of a worshipper during the first world war. 'Mummy, what are they going to do with all these apples?' asks little Peter after attending his first Harvest Thanksgiving. 'They're going to the poor people at the hospital, darling.' PETER (recollecting a recent orgy): 'But I thought people went to the hospital to be *cured* of tummy pain.'

'What Sunday is it?' whispers a wife during divine service in a fashionable church. 'First Sunday after Ascot,' replies her immaculate husband (1923). Away back in 1853, Maria remembers she has forgotten her Prayer Book, just as they reach the church porch. Frederick is properly concerned. 'Well, never mind, dear; but do tell me, is my bonnet straight?' The 'straight and narrow way' of a church aisle was not for those who wore the crinoline. As for the masculine silk hat, might it not be better suspended from the roof by long strings, safe from stray kicks and the dust sacred to every ecclesiastical edifice? No doubt the devotees of fashion would have fortified themselves by quoting Dr. Moffatt's translation (had it existed) of Psalm xxix. 2: 'Worship the Lord in festal attire.' 'Here one goes to Church,' wrote a lady in 1871, 'because lots of people go to the best services.' In those days jaded housemaids rose early and retired late to suit the plans of mistresses whose week-end blended dances and devotion.[1] By the Edwardian period the religious varnish had almost worn off; 'early services' and ritual were no longer a novelty. 'Sunday is an impossible day, about the fullest in the week. . . . We go to Church when it is too wet for golf or motoring.' Sometimes the elderly felt that it was about time they took religion more seriously. This point of view is neatly expressed in Du Maurier's drawing of a man of the world explaining to his grandson why the Church service is at 11 a.m.: 'Ah, my boy, the eleventh hour!'

The type of worship that *Punch* has portrayed for some years past appears to be neither High nor Low, but standardized 'Church of England', whether the sanctuary be in the country or in the West End. The Oxford Movement does not seem to have yet succeeded in abolishing the private pew. People can still be turned out of someone else's pew in the English Church (and other denominations). A lady advances up the aisle, examines an intruder with her monocle and asks: 'Are you Mrs. Pilkington-Haycock?' 'No.' 'Well, I am, and this is my pew.' (1914.) The first world war did not succeed in jolting many people out of the groove of habit, for in 1922 we overhear a retiring pew-opener (pew-doors not quite obsolete!) initiating his successor into the duties: 'Remember, Mr. Higgins, they are very good Christians here until you show someone else into their pew.' Not many pew-holders show

[1] Even in the staid days of Early Victorianism, 'Confirmation Balls' were fashionable, when girls in white rushed into the frivolity they had renounced a few hours before.

the same alacrity in paying a modest subscription to retain their rights, as in repelling intruders. Said one lady of fashion to another: 'Yes, I like the service, but I never enjoy Sunday in the country. I can't bear to think of that pew rent running on at home all the time.'

Punch has always been severe on the parsimony of the rich where the Church is concerned, though he smiles in the most genial way at the small boy who remains in the church porch because the collection is 'beyond my means'. One of Du Maurier's best cartoons shows an elegantly dressed lady avoiding the special collection for the S.P.G. With a deprecating gesture she remarks to the man with the plate, standing outside the porch: 'Oh—er—I'm coming again this afternoon, you know.' After the Afternoon Service, she explains (to a different sidesman): 'Oh—er—I was here this morning, you know.' When one considers that the Church of England is the Church of the richest class in the community, it is a serious criticism of endowments that they encourage even the well-to-do to evade their responsibilities. Voluntary Churches on the other hand, may sometimes feel that it is an uphill fight to be independent, but there is no doubt that the member who gives his 'free-will offering' gladly feels a greater interest in his church, and is obeying in the spirit the New Testament injunction (1 Corinthians, 16$_{1,2}$). References to the offertory in *Punch*, while jocose, have a sting (and rightly so). We watch the Englishman home from the Continent getting rid of his useless small change in the bag. 'All right—I'll pay,' the plutocrat of 1921 signals to his house-party. 'I 'ope everything has been to your likin', sir?' murmurs an ingratiating sidesman as he passes the plate to a worshipper (in private life he is a public waiter and rather absent-minded).

The general impression of church-going gathered from *Punch* is a sense of boredom, varied only by occasional incidents that interest people with reference to their own occupations or hobbies. So when the squire reads the Lesson about Samson catching three hundred foxes and turning them tail to tail, he adds with a sportsman's correctness—'er, that is to say "brush to brush".' The sermon no longer holds the place it did in the Victorian period. In many Anglican congregations it has shrunk to a ten minutes' tonic talk ('pure pelagianism,' says Reinhold Niebuhr, 'despite the Calvinistic *General Confession*'). Punch has never favoured anything approaching sensationalism to arrest attention in the pulpit. Although in favour of good relations between Church and Stage, he believes that their spheres are separate; when Lord Shaftesbury introduced the innovation of services in theatres, the jester ridiculed 'the surplice at the footlights'. He thinks that if the clergy had more human interests, they would hit the target more often.[1] He instances a case to the contrary—a curate preaching to a bored and mystified country flock: 'But, you will quote Eusebius against me!'

Remarks overheard coming out of church are often illuminating. WIFE: 'Did you notice the chinchilla coat on the woman sitting in front?' HUSBAND: 'Er—no. Afraid I was dozing most of the time.' WIFE: 'Um. A lot of good the service did *you*.' Which reminds one of another wife's admonition to her husband at a reception: 'For Goodness' sake don't look at your watch as if you were in church.' Perhaps *Punch* can give the clergy some hints for retaining what remains of their congregations, now that neither fashion nor custom can be counted on. The tradition used to be that the morning service was for the gentry, and the evening service for 'other ranks'. About 1850 evening

---

[1] Even then, you will not please everyone. 'Popular preacher, indeed!' exclaims a woman cleaner to friend, 'I've no patience with 'im. We never 'ad all this mud in the church afore 'e come.'

Communion was introduced to suit working folk and the practice still persists in Evangelical parishes. Evening services seem to be more popular generally than Morning Prayer. The busy housewife and the lazy husband have obviously more time at night; but sometimes there is another reason. 'I am glad to see you come so regularly to our evening service,' said the parson. 'Yus,' replied Mrs. Brown, 'yer see, me 'usband 'ates me goin' hout of a hevening, so I does it to spite 'im.' A tourist in the village inn asks at 7.20 one Sunday evening, in 1922: 'Very quiet tonight, isn't it?' LANDLORD: 'Well, sir, they bean't come out o' Church yet.' Here we have a typically English joke. In North Britain we have 'Sunday closing'—except for the mysterious 'bona-fide traveller' who can get his refreshment at an inn, there is no Scots equivalent to the village inn save the 'bar' to which few need to be 'called'; it would be a most unusual sight to see the frequenters of a Scots 'public' paying a previous visit to the kirk!

We are surprised that more has not been made of the humour of hymnology. The late Dr. Percy Dearmer, in his *Songs of Praise Discussed*, has some amusing pages on the Worm in Hymnology, Hymns for Saints' Days, etc. *Hymns Ancient and Modern* has doubtless humorous aspects which the Victorians would not notice, though the redoubtable Martin Tupper greeted its first appearance with derision (the hymns about heaven seemed to him positively Moslem in their lusciousness). Bernard Partridge allows us to overhear a conversation between a layman and his Vicar, who has recently (1899) introduced Gregorian chants. 'Well, Mr. Rogers, how did you like our music? Tradition says, you know, that those Psalm tunes are the original ones composed by King David.'—'Really? Then I no longer wonder why Saul threw his javelin at him.' A little girl, after attending her first grown-up service (1932) asked: 'Why did the clergyman sing all the time

he was reading? I couldn't hear a word he said.' ELDER
SISTER: 'Hark at her, mummy! He wasn't singing, silly—
he was *intuning in.*' *Punch* laughs off a practice he would
have castigated seventy years ago—but how many 'lis-
teners in' switch off the radio when the service is 'intoned'?

The jester had applauded Disraeli's attempt to put down
ritual in 1874, but when the Revised Prayer Book (1928),
recognizing the ritual developments of half a century, was
rejected by Parliament, he showed none of his old Erastian
and ultra-Protestant fervour. Instead, he represented the
Archbishop of Canterbury standing on a raft (the proposed
Book) driven up and down a sea of Controversy, looking
towards a Lighthouse: *Into haven; a hope that failed.*
Without taking sides, he offers his respectful sympathy to
his Grace.

The issue of High versus Low does not offer much
difficulty to the child mind. An 'infatuated little boy', out
with his clerical father, meets a little girl in the street: 'I
wish you came to our church. Why don't you?' 'Mother
says it's too high.' 'Is that all? Well, I'll speak to Daddy
[in the background] and I'm sure he'll fix that up all right.'
Children's questions about church services are of psychological interest. A little boy is intrigued by the appearance
of the parson at the eagle lectern. 'Oh, gran'ma, what is
he going to do to Polly?' (*The First Lesson.*) A surpliced
choir, predominantly composed of boys, suggests bed-
time (and, to be sure, Episcopal parsons in the more
backward areas of America are known as 'nightgown
preachers'). When one considers the expense of keeping
up an elaborate choral service, there was much point in
Betty's question in Church: 'Mummy, do we get all this
for a penny?' (the 'collection' had just been given).
In 1886 a Sunday-school class was asked, what commandment Adam broke when he took the forbidden fruit? Like
a shot, a small scholar gives the correct answer (which the

teacher never expected)—'Please, sir, th' worn't no commandments then, sir!' The Sunday-school (1914) reveals blank ignorance of the Bible story. 'What do you know about Moses?' 'Please, teacher, it's my first Sunday here and I don't know anybody.' A little girl, who had been told all about Samson, was asked to write a short account of his life. 'I forgot that man's name—so I called him "Archie".' A small boy, passing a hairdresser's on his way home from Sunday-school, remarks—'Going to have my hair cut in here tomorrow.' His chum asks, 'Why don't your mother cut it for you?'—'Me let a woman cut my hair? No fear! Look what happened to Samson!' Whatever may be said of new developments in Religious Education, it is safe to say that abysmal ignorance of the Bible is far more widespread today even among adults of the educated classes. This is true on both sides of the Atlantic. A few years ago *Punch* portrayed an English schoolmaster showing over his school the American mother of a prospective pupil. He concludes: 'I think I may say in the words of the Queen of Sheba, "the half was not told".' AMERICAN MOTHER: 'Say! Has the Queen of Sheba a boy at this school?'

'Well, Bobby,' said the Vicar, 'how's your motor-car?' 'Quite well, thank you,' replies the small boy, 'how's your church?' Compare with this child-like answer the childish reply of an unimaginative uneducated woman to her parson: 'Well, no, sir; I don't seem to get no time to go to church lately. It's different for you, sir, you see, it's your 'obby' (1934). Imagine anyone in the Victorian era (except a professed sceptic) telling a clergyman that church was his hobby! Perhaps there is more in the phrase than meets the eye—over-elaborate services and too many of them, fussy amateurish activities of various kinds. There is a widespread tendency to 'cater for Youth' in such a way that ministers of Christ make their sacred duties marginal,

A CHEERFUL GIVER?

SANDY MCPHERSON, *in a moment of abstraction, put half-a-crown in the collection plate last Sunday in mistake for a penny, and has since expended a deal of thought as to the best way of making up for it.* ' Noo I might stay awa' frae the Kirk till the sum was made up ; but on the ither han' I wad be payin' pew rent a' the time an' gettin' nae guid o' 't.   Losh ! but I'm thinkin' this is what the meenister ca's a " releegious deeficulty ! " '

and 'serve tables' (for which many laymen might be better equipped).

This is foreshadowed by reports of a 'Training Week for Junior Clergy' in the Diocese of Rochester, in which Religion takes a back seat while countless secular activities (physical, recreation, and 'cultural') are well to the fore. A correspondent ('S.J.F.') writes to the *Church Times* in Gilbertian metre:

I am an omnicompetent prefabricated minister,
My versatile dexterity is positively sinister.

.   .   .   .

At singlestick or volley-ball, I'm cool as any icicle,
But very hot on lino-cuts or mending up a bicycle.
My universal chumminess is readily approachable,
And dancing (folk or ballroom) is completely irreproachable.

.   .   .   .

In spite of all my knowledge of the realms of high technology,
I can, if need require, descend to pastoral theology.
But in manifold activities, or dexterous or sinister,
I am the very model of the ultra-modern minister.[1]

These lines give a new turn to the old maxim—*Clerus Anglicanus stupor mundi*. We may hear more of the 'omnicompetent prefabricated minister' if utility becomes the sole virtue of the post-war world, with the result that devotion is despised as 'other-worldly' and scholarship is scouted as 'highbrow'. In certain American circles the Protestant clergy have endeavoured to attune themselves to the life of their community so much that they have become purveyors of miscellaneous information, 'uplift', and entertainment rather than ambassadors of Christ. *Punch* would do well to show up the would-be 'omnicom-

[1] With acknowledgements, also, to *The London Quarterly and Holborn Review* (Editorial—July, 1944).

petent prefabricated minister' as 'a jack of all trades and master of none'. In the past the fanatic, the pedant, and the aesthete have had short shift. It is now the turn of the man who plays to the gallery and is willing to do anything to make the Church popular, whether by 'catering for Youth' or by identifying the Kingdom of God with the party programme of those who promise most in their 'New Order'.

Looking backwards through the arches of the years, what is the general impression of *Punch's* influence on the religion of Great Britain since his first appearance in 1841? The national jester has been a national historian. In his earlier days he spoke confidently for England and claimed to touch every spring of social life. The fact that he identified himself wholeheartedly with predominant national convictions makes him a true mirror of passing modes of thought and feeling. Undoubtedly he was sometimes in the wrong. As regards public men in Church or State he was too ready to see their characters as either black or white; he either admired or detested. Cardinal Wiseman had a touch of ostentation that doubtless called for correction, but he was one of the most learned and accomplished men of his era and did not deserve to be pelted with abuse. Bishop Samuel Wilberforce had an oleaginous streak in his character, but surely his wit might have covered a multitude of sins (when asked by a child why he was called 'Soapy Sam', he explained: 'Because I have so much dirty work to do and I always come out of it with clean hands.').[1] Abraham Lincoln was a 'real human' whose idiosyncrasies afforded ample occasion for humour, but surely not for sneers that helped to embitter our relationship with the United States. *Punch* was free from indelicacy, but his invective was often coarse and unfair. Thus he

[1] For instances of his ready wit, see P. H. Ditchfield, *The Old-Time Parson*, pp. 68–75 (Methuen, 1908).

gave publicity to the wildly exaggerated fears of 'papal aggression' in 1850; surely the Church of Rome had the right to call their 'Vicars Apostolic' bishops, in a free country. It was hardly fair to assume that every monastery and nunnery was a sink of iniquity. Whether the 'Ritualists' were right or wrong is a matter of personal opinion, but the majority were certainly not camouflaged emissaries of the Pope.

To get the right perspective, we must understand that in the middle of the nineteenth century the English Church was essentially a national institution, closely bound up with the Constitution; it must therefore reflect, not the passing fashions in theology and modes of worship, but the settled traditions of the English people. We have seen that *Punch* was concerned about the low standard of clerical efficiency,[1] and how he condemned vested interests bound up with the Church in alliance with class ascendancy. Complete Erastian that he was, he failed to realize that the dead hand of the State could never regenerate a moribund Church; Satan could never cast out Satan. Nevertheless, *Punch* did play a decisive part in laughing out of existence many of the evils that discredited the Church and lessened its usefulness. He stood for the removal of Nonconformist disabilities, though he disliked 'the Nonconformist Conscience'—so bound by taboos, rigid asceticism, and sectarian ethics. He opposed the emancipation of the Jews, but was apparently ashamed of his unfairness and afterwards rallied to the support of this unhappy race. He disliked Evangelicals, but had to admit that they were a potent spiritual leaven in the Established Church. He ridiculed the cause of Missions, but he honoured Missionary heroes. His humanitarian

---

[1] In 1845, 2,000 inhabitants of Rochdale petitioned Parliament that the hanging of criminals should be done by a clergyman. *Punch* suggested an appropriate advertisement for *The Times*: 'Wanted, a clergyman in every way fitted for the gallows.'

FLIPPANT

VICAR (*who has introduced 'Gregorian' tones into his service*). 'Well, Mr. Rogers, how did you like our music? Tradition says, you know, that those Psalm tunes are the original ones composed by King David.'

PARISHIONER. 'Really? then I no longer wonder why Saul threw his javelin at him!'

enthusiasm supported those Americans who tried to confine slavery within the limits of certain States: 'Thus far shall Slavery go; no farther. That tide must ebb from this time forth.' When the Civil War broke out and the South put up a gallant fight, *Punch* was swung round by the pseudo-romantic sentiment that saw the planters as 'cavaliers'. Generally, however, despite lapses and inconsistency, we may claim the national jester as the ardent advocate of justice and humanity at home and abroad.

At the end of the Gladstonian era, broadly speaking, we can detect a change in *Punch's* attitude. He became more conservative in public affairs, an 'Imperialist'. He retired from theological and ecclesiastical controversy, leaving it to the clergy.[1] Abuses having been reformed in the Church,[2] he ceases to be an 'anti-clerical'. This attitude becomes more marked when the twentieth century is reached. Is it the effect of a kindly mellowing in old age? Or is it rather a tacit recognition that Religion does not interest a wide section of the British public when it is presented in the form of instruction, eulogy, admonition, and castigation? The Church is no longer the 'sure-fire' topic it once was. Without taking up a partisan attitude, I venture to suggest that it is a pity to represent organized religion almost exclusively by the inept remarks of pompous parsons, raw curates, pious spinsters, illiterate villagers and subservient vergers.

The Church is supposed to be always behind the times, but even ecclesiastically we have moved out of the kind of world you so often picture, *Mr. Punch*, and we would like a little more freshness, and a few indications that Chris-

---

[1] Some would contend he became 'pro-clerical', e.g. in his attitude to Church Schools; in the middle of the nineteenth century he had advocated national and non-sectarian education.

[2] A diocesan inspector asks a class, "Explain 'Honour' in the fifth commandment." The boy replies: "Please, sir, they don't teach us DOGMA in our school" (1906).

tianity is alive and kicking, and not simply a survival from
a vanished social scene. It is not unfair criticism to say that
you still view life too much through the spectacles of the
upper and professional classes.[1] You ignore what they
ignore—for instance, the Free Churches; their contribution
to the life of England should be generously recognized and
tactful treatment would help to put an end to their
'inferiority complex': and you make no attempt to enlighten
English ignorance of that national institution, the Kirk of
Scotland, which still appears in distorted music-hall guise!
Here, too, there is much room for improvement.

While recommending that *Punch* should not altogether
give up his old office of reformer (without being too
officious) we admit that reformers are apt to be 'viewy' and
take themselves too seriously. Protesters against tradition,
they may become thralls to some 'ism. The jester's grain
of salt is an invaluable preservative against stale tradition
and tendentious theory. Perfectly sincere religious people
sometimes lack the 'saving' sense of humour that gives
breadth and humanity to their religion. Apparently trivial
sayings and incidents are often of unsuspected psychological
importance. 'Whenever [men] wax out of proportion,'
says George Meredith, 'whenever they offend sound reason
and fair justice, are false in humility or mined with conceit,
individually or in the bulk—the Spirit overhead will look
humanely malign and cast an oblique light on them,
followed by volleys of silvery laughter. That is the Comic
Spirit' (essay on the comic spirit).

It is refreshing to note that when *Mr. Punch's* Jubilee
was celebrated in 1891, a service was held in commemora-

[1] Yet one can sympathize with their domestic difficulties.
Punch cites a recent 'Lost Cause'. "Housekeeper reqd. by
clergyman of the University, to manage small house; someone
who understands proper care of silver, etc., and the ways of the
real upper classes, and would be likely to become a friend and
old family servant."—Advt. in *Oxford Times*.

tion. This 'religious exercise' (quite unofficial) was conducted by the Rev. J. de Kewer Williams. 'I led my people yesterday, in giving thanks on the occasion of your Jubilee, praying that you might ever be as discreet and kindly as you have always been.' The pulpit prayer for *Punch* ended as follows: 'It is so easy to be witty and wicked, and so hard to be witty and wise. May its satire ever be as good and genial, and the other papers follow its excellent example!'

In 1946 we might well join again in this prayer for *Punch*, adding to it a verse inscribed on one of the walls of Chester Cathedral:

> Give me a sense of humour, Lord,
> Give me grace to see a joke,
> To get some happiness from life,
> And pass it on to other folk.

BLIND GUIDES

OLD GENTLEMAN.   'Very charming old sedilia you have here.'
CARETAKER.   'Yes, sir, you ain't by no means the fust as 'as admired 'em. That's where the clergymen used to sit, in the order of their senility.'